Man at Work

400 Years in Paintings and Bronzes
Labor and the Evolution of Industry in Art

Anonymous: Four Workers in Front of a Furnace, oil on canvas, 36×30 in., signed

Man at Work

400 Years in Paintings and Bronzes

Labor and the Evolution of Industry in Art

Klaus Türk

The Eckhart G. Grohmann Collection
at Milwaukee School of Engineering

 MSOE Press, Milwaukee, Wisconsin

Man at Work
400 Years in Paintings and Bronzes
Labor and the Evolution of Industry in Art

© 2003 Milwaukee School of Engineering. All rights reserved.

Text: Klaus Türk, Wuppertal, Germany
Assistance: Hans Peter Linckh, Arnold Linckh and Peter Benecke

Photography: Paul W. Roberts, Milwaukee School of Engineering, Milwaukee, Wisconsin
              Larry Sanders, Milwaukee, Wisconsin

Layout, image processing and composition: Klaus Türk

Translations: Eckhart G. Grohmann, Aluminum Casting and Engineering Co., Milwaukee, Wisconsin
               Hermann Viets, Ph.D., Milwaukee School of Engineering, Milwaukee, Wisconsin

Publisher: Milwaukee School of Engineering
               1025 North Broadway, Milwaukee, Wisconsin 53202, USA
               (414) 277-7173
               www.bookstore.msoe.edu
               Director of Publications: Leigh Ann Hass

Distribution of the German edition by Klartext Verlagsgesellschaft mbH, Essen, Germany
         Email: info@klartext-verlag.de
         www.klartext-verlag.de

ISBN   0-9128044-0-4 (English Edition)
         3-89861-209-0 (German Edition)

Printed in the United States of America by Inland Press/Inland Book, Menomonee Falls, Wisconsin

Foreword

by Hermann Viets, Ph.D.
President *Milwaukee School of Engineering*

By simply picking up this very substantial book, the reader will be impressed by the size and breadth of the ECKHART G. GROHMANN COLLECTION. Examining the book will build on that impression of scale with a concept of quality. Finally, reading the history and descriptions will allow the reader to appreciate the uniqueness and value of this wonderful collection.

To understand the ECKHART G. GROHMANN COLLECTION it is helpful to understand Dr. Grohmann. His family background includes a large marble processing and quarry business in Silesia, close to the German-Polish and Czech borders. It was there that he developed his appreciation and admiration of hard work, a concept repeatedly found in these pages. Hard work to Eckhart Grohmann is not an idealized concept but a principle for his life.

Dr. Grohmann is a multifaceted entrepreneur. He has built a number of very successful companies, including a leading company in the highly competitive aluminum casting industry, while simultaneously nurturing an intense interest in art. Dr. Grohmann is an expert on the paintings of Carl Spitzweg, and a well-known collector of genre art. This collection of industrial art was acquired over a period of 35 years while working hard to build his businesses and collections. Having built a truly unique *Man at Work* collection, Dr. Grohmann debated in his own mind where such a collection would have the greatest positive impact. Would it be in a traditional museum or in a nontraditional setting? Where was the primary audience for these works and where would they be most appreciated? Dr. Grohmann chose a nontraditional location for his nontraditional collection. He recognized the pragmatic approach of the *Milwaukee School of Engineering* as an educational analogy to the *Man at Work* collection. He saw the benefit of his collection in the university context as not only providing the students a very valuable exposure to art, but also an historical context for their own studies. All that our students learn, they build on the efforts of others. Many of these efforts are illustrated in this volume. Our understanding of metallurgy, for example, evolved from the illustrated blast furnaces in the 1600s. Our factories, first driven literally by manpower and horsepower, and later by water and steam, evolved into those powered by electricity. This evolution of industry is not accidental but rather composed of doing, learning and redoing. The ECKHART G. GROHMANN COLLECTION clearly shows our dependence on our predecessors for all we know and for our existence itself.

The beneficiaries of Dr. Grohmann's generosity are the MSOE students, faculty and staff as well as all of those who will be exposed to this collection through visits or outreach activities, such as this book. The ECKHART G. GROHMANN COLLECTION at *Milwaukee School of Engineering* will continue to teach history, technology and art to future generations. They will learn of the sophistication of industry even hundreds of years ago, and the talents of those who chronicled these activities.

On behalf of the *Milwaukee School of Engineering*, I thank Dr. Grohmann for his generous gift. It will be of ongoing value to all of MSOE, particularly our students. Personally, I thank him for the opportunity to participate in the planning and production of this volume. It has been a pleasure and privilege to work with him.

INTRODUCTION

by Eckhart G. Grohmann, D.E. (hon.)
MSOE Regent
Chairman and President *Aluminum Casting & Engineering Company* (ACE/CO)

Each of us is the product of our birth and the environment in which we grow. As a young boy, I watched the tradesmen working in our family marble enterprise in the former state of Silesia in Eastern Germany. I watched the blacksmiths, carpenters, quarry workers, stone cutters, and especially the master sculptors and their apprentices create marble statues for monuments and elaborate tombstones.

The end of WWII changed all of that. Poland was permitted to annex my home state of Silesia and disowned and expelled the civilian German population. As did many others, my family fled as refugees and resettled in West Germany. After obtaining a sound education there, I came to the United States and was offered an opportunity to enter the metalworking industry in 1965 with the *Aluminum Casting & Engineering Company* in Milwaukee. This small aluminum foundry developed into a considerable enterprise today, making large-volume aluminum components for the automotive industry. During these changes, my admiration and deep respect for the hard work of individuals – be it as foundryworkers, stonecutters or any other working career – has remained. These individuals have always been intriguing and fascinating to me.

Starting in the 1960s, I have been searching for artwork depicting industry and individual workers and craftsmen in their workplaces. Early success finding a painting of a blacksmith or a statue of a foundryworker started a passion for collecting interesting pieces on the subject of "man at work."

My exposure to the *Milwaukee School of Engineering (MSOE)* since 1974, first as a Corporation member and later as a Regent, caused me to realize the value of the subject of work to young people. They study modern technology, usually without having had the opportunity of an apprenticeship or an exposure to the fundamental importance of the basic trades to today's automated production processes. An idea developed to expose the collection to our young MSOE students, thereby opening their eyes to the historical evolution of work from its early and modest beginnings. This will allow them to better understand the roots of today's modern production process.

A unique opportunity presented itself by meeting Dr. Klaus Türk, a sociology professor at the *University of Wuppertal,* who has studied the "man at work" theme his entire life. He had just published the most comprehensive book about images of human work, *Bilder der Arbeit,* in 2000. Professor Türk's experience in organizing the collection and developing the historical context in his comprehensive introductory chapter is invaluable to appreciating and understanding the subject matter in its entirety.

Some of the material will be incorporated into the MSOE curriculum to allow the students a better understanding of history and an elementary appreciation of industrial art.

In addition to the book, study materials will be available to the students in electronic format to enjoy at leisure. The planned future conversion of the historic *German-English Academy* building into a campus museum with an audio guide will increase the exposure of the MSOE students to the artwork by encouraging frequent visits. My hope is that this collection will augment and enrich the strenuous education now provided by the technical university.

I hope not only the student body, but also the MSOE faculty, alumni, friends of the university and eventually the public, will enjoy visiting the past to better appreciate today's resulting high standard of living.

Contents

HISTORICAL REVIEW: LABOR AND INDUSTRY IN ART

by Klaus Türk

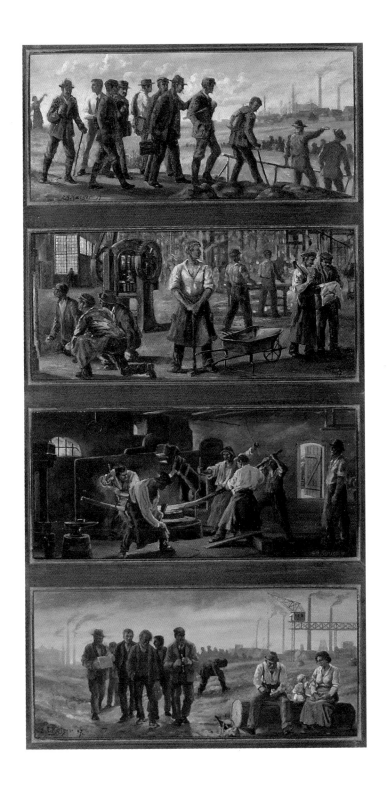

Kaiser, E.A.: Workers' World, 4 panels, 32.5×16 in., 1937, signed, the ECKHART G. GROHMANN COLLECTION

The paintings and bronzes of the ECKHART G. GROHMANN COLLECTION come from a broad historical stream of artwork on the subject of human labor and industry. Therefore we start with a short introductory overview on the historical imagery of work and industry, followed by the collection itself.

HISTORICAL REVIEW

Humans are not the only species to develop communication. However, only humans have developed art as well as labor. Art and labor allows them to create their own reality and to interact with it. So humans alone possess the ability to responsively monitor and structure their world.

It follows from this, that both art and work are necessarily historical phenomena and that they have a strong correlation to one another. For this reason it is of special interest to study those aspects of art, which reflect the world of work. Ever since the dawn of history men have depicted their own labors. Hunting scenes dominate prehistoric cave drawings. Egyptians employed tomb drawings and sculptures to illustrate the building of the pyramids. The tradition continued with the Greeks and Romans documenting their daily activities with a wide variety of visual treasures.

As human artifacts, pictures are an early and wonderful source of historical information. But what kind of information can the pictures provide? The answer to this question is more complex than to naively assume that the pictures provide an accurate recording of reality. More than a reflection of precise reality, paintings create something

new, a reconstruction and interpretation of contemporary reality. Recognizing this fact raises the question of realism of the paintings.

In this context, which image is more "realistic"— that created by Hermann Heijenbrock [1] or that by Gerd Arntz [2]? At first glance the choice may be Heijenbrock because he depicts what we believe to represent the accurate physical reality. But with more contemplation, is not the woodcut by Arntz more realistic because, beyond the physical, it better represents the more general conditions and atmosphere of the factory?

Both artists would insist that they correctly represent their subject. But a totally objective representation is not possible. Arntz and Heijenbrock each

[1] Heijenbrock, Herman: Steel Mill at Hörde, Germany, 1913

ignore what the other emphasizes. Neither artist is neutral, each striving to represent the subject in his own manner. Therefore, determining historical accuracy from paintings is not an easy task. All paintings have a story to tell, but that story remains for us to discover. To reveal that story, the following questions may be helpful:

1) What clues can we extract concerning the methods by which goods were produced? Which technologies were employed and under what conditions? To what extent are the paintings historical documents of the material means and conditions of production?

2) What can we learn of the cultural and societal environments in which the paintings were produced, including the political context? To what degree are the paintings ideological and political documents?

3) What can the paintings tell us about the history of art as a medium of expression? How do they illustrate the artistic forms and matters of interpretation of work and industry?

Seldom are these questions raised relative to the art of work and industry. The objective of this volume of the ECKHART G. GROHMANN COLLECTION at the *Milwaukee School of Engineering* is to stimulate additional interest and research in this area of work.

Our historical overview begins with the European Middle Ages.

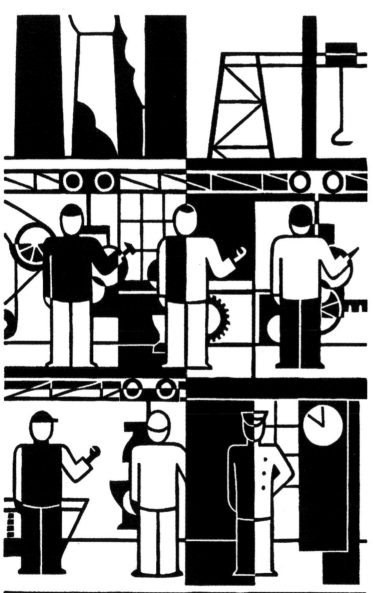

[2] Arntz, Gerd: Factory, 1927

Note: The pictures in this chapter are not from the ECKHART G. GROHMANN COLLECTION.

12

A Brief History of Labor Imagery

Images of work in the Middle Ages serve both as an illustration in written texts and as an alternative to text for an illiterate population. The picture of work is usually cast in a religious or moral context. Work does not yet appear as an independent subject, but rather is deeply embedded into daily life or even is daily life itself, at least for the working class majority. In medieval society, this majority was dominated by the political and spiritual demands of its rulers.

By long tradition, work is illustrated through annual aides, called "pictures of the month" [3]. These cycles are usually integrated with an astrologic cosmology and incorporate the seasonal agricultural activities. The aides represent both calendars and humans deeply embedded in eternal, God-given cycles of life. This repetitive structure is sometimes depicted in round pictures (for example, calendar disks) reflecting the static, repetitive, change-resistant world of the Middle Ages. Nevertheless, the European Middle Ages did produce a number of technical innovations, some of them shown in the chronological bar (see also [5]).

The Catholic Church dominated the society and culture of the Middle Ages. Depictions of work are common in prayer books and Biblical illustrations of the period, beginning with the Genesis "…with the sweat of your brow shall you eat of your bread" [4]. The subject of Adam and Eve at work continues throughout many centuries. Here work appears as a God-ordained requirement rather than a historical or societal activity. This led to a division of work between the sexes, illustrated in the New Testament by the appearance of the Holy Family at work. Eve and Mary are often shown spinning, weaving or raising

[3] Medieval Calendar: July, August, September, ca. 809

[4] Grandval Bible: Expulsion From Paradise, ca. 1350

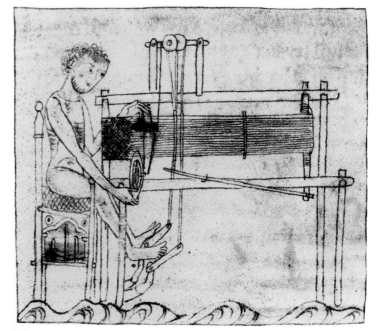

[5] British Miniature: Weaver With Treadle Loom, ca. 1250

800	1000	1200
Middle Ages ⇨ rise of feudalism harness for horses and oxen	water wheel with camshaft plow with leading wheel	windmill	foot-activated loom wooden flail

children. Meanwhile, Adam and Joseph are engaged in fieldwork or carpentry. However, the Biblical work themes offer recurring opportunities to encourage the positive attributes of work and to present new technologies. Many contemporary depictions of the familiar Tower of Babel story emphasize not the original lesson but rather the very process of building. For example, [6] illustrates a foot-activated crane and a *devil's claw* on the right (see also pages 300/301).

Finally, the splendid Gothic prayer books of the nobility show both the technical methods of production as well as the societal framework. For example, [7] shows a plow with a lead wheel (a technical innovation) in the foreground, while the ruler's castle oversees the scene from the background. Thus the societal context of authority is interpreted and legitimated as cosmological fact.

[6] Bible of Wenzel: Construction of the Tower of Babel, ca. 1390

[7] Prayerbook of the Duke of Berry: March, ca. 1413

1300			1450
spinning wheel	gear-driven clock with weights	peak period of trade guilds	iron cannon balls
strong importance of merchant capital in cities	iron casting, blast furnaces		

The concept of work changed as the end of the 15th century approached, due to the great cultural revolution of the times (Renaissance, Reformation, discovery of new lands and colonization). The changes are reflected in the images of work the era produced. Worldly figures, independent of religion, appear in books of trades and artisans as well as in illustrated manuscripts. The development of trade capitalism and the resulting increased dependence on money resulted in critical depictions of greed and profit, as well as the earliest portraits of wealthy merchants.

By the first half of the 16th century, paintings of preindustrial plants emerge, as seen in the Patenier school (see the illustration in the next chapter). Protestant Holland was the first to find it worthy to depict the everyday world of work. Two retirement homes to care for elderly craftsmen were established by charities in the German trading center of Nuremberg. The residents of these homes have been portrayed in their former trades and professions over a period of 300 years, providing a rich basis of source material for the study of work [8].

Over the course of the 16th century, a complete transition occurred in the concept of work. By the century's end a new concept of work as an independent subject was propagated in many paintings. Work was now viewed as a separate sphere of human effort and became a means of "industrification" (industry in the true sense of industriousness) of men. From now

[8] Mendelsche Zwölfbrüderstiftung: Rowel Maker, 1457

[9] Agricola, Georg: Water Conveyor, 1556

1450		1500
Age of Renaissance ⇨	Leonardo da Vinci	benchvice
printing with moveable types (Gutenberg 1452)	Reformation	"discovery" of America

on labor could be treated as an object of mechanization, rationalization and organization.

The mercantilistic and technological view of work is found in many allegories, emblems and a series of books on (technological) trades. An increasing number of scientific books with mechanical descriptions appear at this time, especially books on mining [9]. These books signal the onset of a new period. The conflict is between the well-ordered system of traditional trades and a developing system organizing the trades into a factorylike setting generally supported by the arising modern state. A famous example is the German *Book of the Trades* (*Ständebuch*) by Jost Amman [10] of Nuremberg. Yet in the context of the state and guilds, work still is seen as being provided by God and hence, serving God. The guild books make the hierarchy of the trades very clear. The books reflect the cultural, political and cooperative lifestyle of the 16th-century tradespeople, organized into units. With this background, the new prefactory business community continued to evolve and prosper.

The contemporary 16th-century technical publications show an increasing independence from religion. The extensive and illustrated work on mining by Georg Agricola in 1556 [9] is a wonderful example of scientific and engineering accomplishment and was translated from Latin to English by future President Herbert Hoover and his wife, Lou Henry Hoover. Only 200 copies were published in 1912. This was soon followed by the series *Nova Reperta* (new discoveries) by Stradanus, celebrating the technological advances of this new era ([11] shows one plate of the series).

[10] Amman, Jost: The Weaver, 1568

[11] Stradanus, Johannes: Sugar Production, 1570

1550		1600
pocketwatch (Henlein, 1510)	"guild registry" by J. Amman (1567)	loom for producing stockings
treadle-driven spinning wheel	mining book by Agricola (1556) microscope	first org. labor in penitentiaries

In the following (17th) century, the concept of work continued to evolve in the direction of ever more organized industrial activity. Simultaneously, traditional work, particularly farming, became a major subject of the genre paintings in the Netherlands, partly as satire but also as critical realism (i.e., Brueghel, ter Borch, Ostade).

Both the beginning of rationalism and advent of the modern political state occurred in Europe during the baroque period. The landowning aristocracy established and controlled centralized locations to produce luxury goods as well as war materials. These organized facilities were increasingly competitive relative to the traditional handcrafts. *Labor omnia vincit* (hard work prevails), an adapted quote from the Roman poet Virgil, was their slogan. The labor was still handwork and not yet organized in the manner of later factories.

The *Book of the Trades* by Christoph Weigel of 1698 was the first major, comprehensive, illustrated text on mercantilism, describing 204 trades [12]. It no longer placed the clergy in the forefront, as Amman did, but rather focused on the reality of worldly power, such as the military and the weapons trade. The context of work was now to benefit the state, or more precisely, to benefit the state treasury for the purpose of war.

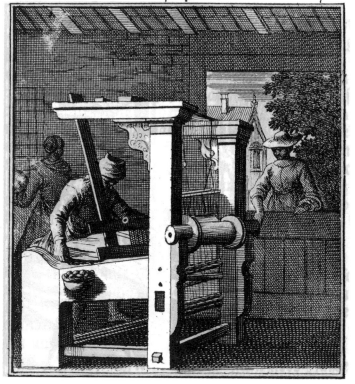

[12] Weigel, Christoph: The Weaver, 1698

[13] Le Nain, Louis: A Farrier in his Forge, ca. 1640

1600		1650
Baroque Age ⇨	1618 - 1648 30 Year War in Europe	rationalism (Descartes) and empiricalism (Bacon)
1612 tobacco farming in North America	first slaves in North America	1642 calculator (Pascal)

In the arising new process of work organization, a group of skilled craftsmen would be organized by a wealthy person to work in what might resemble a factory. The skilled individuals would work either in a factory or separately at their homes but would be paid a wage and have no ownership in their production (so-called putting-out system). Thus they worked like a craftsman and were paid like an employee. Very often the representative of the state, the aristocratic ruler, would own the production facility (manufacturer). Later changes resulted in a factory where various individuals' efforts were integrated to produce a product.

The brothers Le Nain [13] developed a concept of "secular holiness" with their paintings of mythological reality, an effect later found in the work of Jean-François Millet and Vincent van Gogh. The Spanish artist Diego Velázquez [14] used the mythological tale of the weaving competition between the Goddess Pallas Athene and Arachne in his painting *The Spinning Women* in order to place the court's industrious work in the foreground as if on a stage. Velázquez continued to experiment with different levels of reality in many of his other paintings.

[14] Velázquez, Diego: The Spinning Women, ca. 1657

| 1640/63 air pump (v. Guericke) | Isaac Newton (1643-1727) cottage industries | 1690 basic steam engine (Papin) |

The process of making work more efficient and rational is found in the extensive and richly illustrated publications on household management. Their objective was to develop rules to guide the efficient patriarchal management of household and family. Thus, the new definition of work had evolved into a pedagogical activity continuing into the 18th century.

Success of the early ventures led to increasing capital investments and hence an acceleration in the development of industrial technology. As a result, the output of the organized craft facilities significantly increased. This new organization of work spread to workhouses and penal and mental institutions. In 1700, London had about 40 workhouses, while the imperial wool facility in Linzm, Austria, employed about 26,000 people. The pedagogical activity is impressively personified by the illustrated *Industry and Idleness* by William Hogarth [15]. This tale contrasts one ambitious and one lazy weaver boy. At the end of the tale, the ambitious boy becomes the Lord Mayor of London while the lazy boy awaits execution. The lessons are often repeated in literature, later resulting in the tale of *Horatio Alger* in the United States.

The Industrial Revolution began about 1750 in Great Britain. Demand and scale led to rapid capitalistic growth, especially in the textile and iron industries. As subjects of paintings, industrial work processes are slowly and hesitantly embraced by the art community. Thus, Joseph Wright of Derby, England, although motivated by technological progress, still chose to paint traditional processes in his series on blacksmiths

[15] Hogarth, William: Industry and Idleness, Plate 1, 1747

[16]. He placed them into a mystical setting, much as the Le Nain brothers did. To the left is a man deep in thought while the figure of the woman reminds us of the popular subject of the visit of Venus to the force of Vulcan (see the work of Brueghel within

[16] Wright of Derby, Joseph: The Iron Forge (detail), 1772

1700		**1750**
Age of Enlightenment and the Industrial Revolution ⇨		1700 potato farming in England
1718 mercury thermometer (Fahrenheit)	1735 production of iron using only coke	1742 cast steel

the ECKHART G. GROHMANN COLLECTION). The mysterious atmosphere is enhanced by the treatment of light and shadow.

At this point, it was still advantageous to have a special event to precipitate a painting of a work process. The earliest painters of this genre, Swede Pehr Hilleström [17] and Belgian Léonard Defrance [18] often used the occasion of an aristocratic visit to the shop as motivation, but yet placed the work and production processes, and not the visitor, at the center of their compositions. Defrance, a participant in the French Revolution, painted small format interiors of factories and iron working plants, mostly commissioned by the entrepreneurs responsible for the development of these businesses. He did not shy away from depicting the miserable working conditions, such as the child labor in the tobacco factories.

Pehr Hilleström, painter to the Swedish Royal Court, depicted the king's holdings in more than a hundred oil paintings. His paintings emphasized the working conditions and are considered to have had a strong influence on the course of industrial art.

[17] Hilleström, Pehr: Charge Platform of a Furnace at Berkinge Near Forsmark Bruk, 1792

[18] Defrance, Léonard: Interior of a Hammer Mill, ca. 1780

1800

1767 Spinning Jenny (Hargreaves)	1769 Flyer Spinning Jenny (Arkwright)	1774/79 Mule Twist Spinning Jenny (Crompton)
1776 steam engine in iron work	1784 puddle method	1789/90 steam-powered iron rolling mills

In the middle of the 19th century, the image of work made a breakthrough. Even though farming remained the popular theme of the middle class *biedermeyer* (rather conservative) imagination, French artists Gustave Courbet and Jean François Millet [19] challenged this theme in 1848 with a "new realism." Some of their paintings triggered scandals and protests because they pushed traditional aesthetic boundaries, despite Millet's deeply religious relationship to land and its use. Several years later, Vincent van Gogh admired and adopted many of Millet's working themes.

[20] Hübner, Karl Wilhelm: The Silesian Weavers, 1844

[19] Millet, Jean-François: The Sower, 1850; © 2002 Museum of Fine Arts, Boston

In Germany, Karl Wilhelm Hübner dared to create a unique painting for these times – one accusing the capitalists of refusing to accept the homemade production of the traditional cottage weavers [20]. During those days, German weavers revolted against exploitation by capitalists, especially those in Silesia.

Landscape paintings continued to show more and more industrial installations until industrial portraits evolved. The belching smokestack became the symbol for industrial productivity, wealth and power. There was a growth of art depicting industrial production processes, and a slow evolution from visual impressionism to a visual analysis of space, machinery and labor.

The initial large oil paintings of this type were created by John Ferguson Weir in the USA and François Bonhommé in France. Weir was commissioned by the president of the West Point Foundry to paint the casting of the *Parrot cannon* [21], which was deployed in the American Civil War (this subject was also used for a stained glass panel, see p. 84). A second painting, *Forging the Shaft*, was created in 1867. It was destroyed by fire and recreated 10 years later.

1800		1850
Age of Manufacturing ⇨ 1814 mechanical cotton loom (Lowell)	1826 sewing machine	1826 ship propeller (Ressels)
1829 steam locomotive "Rocket" (Stevenson)	1839 steam forge (Nasmyth)	1847 cast steel cannon (Krupp)

François Bonhommé was the first modern painter of European industry. In the 1850s and '60s he worked in the heavy industrial plants of the Schneider Corporation in Le Creusot, France. He drew and painted industrial workers and industrial landscapes with very unusual perspectives and production processes as seen in [22], where huge ship crankshafts are forged. Some of the finished product is shown in the foreground of the painting. Workers and machinery form a common entity; the individuality of the worker is dwarfed by the huge production equipment. No longer does one see the individual executing a work assignment in the traditional sense. Rather, modern industry is depicted as a combination of dominating technology and human labor.

[21] Weir, John Ferguson: The Gun Foundry, 1866; Putnam County Historical Society Museum, Cold Spring, N.Y.

[22] Bonhommé, François: Forgeage au mateau-pilon dans les ateliers d'Indret de l'arbre coude d'une frégate de 600 cv (Forging a Crankshaft for a Ship), 1865

1870

1855 steel production with Bessemer vessel 1859/69 Suez Canal 1859 start of oil drilling in the USA 1861 telephone (Reis)
1863 rotating press 1864 Siemens-Martin Process in steel production 1867 reinforced concrete (Monier), dynamite (Nobel)

The period 1870 to 1945 can be called the principal era of art depicting work. The modern "working society" was developed, and the artists participated in the debate over its meaning.

The new recognition of women represented a controversial subject. The traditional painters never tired of depicting women in the "quiet labor" of textile handwork. The new social realism (i.e., Max Liebermann, see his picture in the ECKHART G. GROHMANN COLLECTION) placed the hard and socially low-esteemed work of women at the center – until then an unthinkable subject in pictorial art circles.

In Germany, Adolph Menzel painted the famous *Eisenwalzwerk* (*Iron Rolling Mill*) in 1872/75

[23] Menzel, Adolph: The Iron Rolling Mill, 1872/75

[24] Anshutz, Thomas Pollock [American, 1851-1912]: The Iron Workers' Noontime, oil on canvas, 17×23.8 in., 1880/81

Imperialism/Unrestrained Capitalism ⇨ 1876 four-cycle gas engine   1876 telephone (Bell)
1876 ammonia refrigeration machine (Linde)   1879 introduction of the electrical carbon fiber lightbulb (Edison)

[23]. It depicts the hard work required in the most advanced rolling mill for railroad tracks in Königshütte in the East German industrial area of Silesia (annexed to Poland after WWI and WWII). While combining the atmosphere with the depiction of hard working conditions, it makes no reference to the bitter labor battles occurring in Silesia at that time. The painting will be copied for the ECKHART G. GROHMANN COLLECTION in the near future (for more details see pages 214/215).

The physical strength of the worker is the main thrust of the painting by Menzel, as well as Thomas Pollock Anshutz [24]. The iron workers base their self-confidence as a group on the quality of their bodies, here pampered in the sun.

The violent labor conflicts in all capitalistic countries were now shown in oil paintings for the first time. In France and Belgium, for example, the artists Alfred Philippe Roll and Jules Adler created paintings of strike scenes. German-American Robert Koehler painted a dramatic scene of a strike for equitable pay in the Belgian city of Charleroi [25]. Particularly in this industrially advanced country, an intense artistic confrontation evolved with industrial labor. The most distinguished protagonist was Constantin Meunier, who will be further described in the later chapters dealing with the ECKHART G. GROHMANN COLLECTION.

[25] Koehler, Robert: The Strike, 1886

1882 electric power plant in New York   1883 punch card machine (Hollerith)   violent labor conflicts in capitalistic countries
1893 photocell (Elster/Geitel)   1895 cinematography (Lumière)   first assembly line production in USA

The artistic criticism of modern work further differentiated itself toward the end of the 19th century with a search for new forms. A socially critical realism evolved to confront the traditional industrial painting, for example, Käthe Kollwitz, Sella Hasse, Hans Baluschek in Germany and Théophile Steinlen in France.

Industrial painting developed its own genre including some highly developed commercial production studios. Several artists focused solely on depicting work and particularly industry (i.e., Leonard Sandrock, Herman Heijenbrock, Otto Bollhagen and later on Erich Mercker, the work of each will appear later in this volume). It became increasingly appealing to corporations to decorate their boardrooms, executive offices and company publications with industrial art. Many paintings and sculptures were commissioned by entrepreneurs.

The high esteem in which industrial art was held is demonstrated in early art exhibits organized with this theme. An example is the 100th anniversary of the *Friedrich Krupp Corporation* in Germany in 1912. Otto Bollhagen created a large series of paintings of the *Krupp* factories commissioned for this event, among them the painting *Tiegelstahlguss (Steel Foundry)* [26]. As are almost all of the paintings of

[26] Bollhagen, Otto: Crucible Casting in the Old Melting Furnace of the Gussstahlfabrik Friedr. Krupp at Essen about 1890, 1912

1900

Imperialism/High Capitalism ⇨ 1901 first flights with motor-powered airplane (Whitehead)   1903 motor-powered flight of Wright Brothers   1904 vacuum tube, diode (Flemming)   1906 gas turbine   1906 diesel locomotive

this series, *Tiegelstahlguss* is extraordinary due to the choice of perspective used to illustrate the monumental size of the Krupp production complex.

The period around the turn of the 20th century is marked by the parallel events of the rapid growth of both the industrial production facilities and the imperial political ambitions of the national states. For instance, the American gross national product increased seven times during the last third of the 19th century. Industry, with its productivity and efficiency, often received great praise. The power of nations was now based on the productivity of their economies and their capability for war production. The dominating ideology of productive power raised energy and power to the highest priority. Many works of art express this guiding ideal, as in the paintings of Frenchman Victor Tardieu [27].

The other, dark side of extreme capitalism was the issue of monumental

[28] Stella, Joseph: In the Glare of the Converter, 1909

[27] Tardieu, Victor: Work, 1902; Musée des Beaux-Arts de Rennes

social problems, especially in the concentrated industrial centers. Motivated by this phenomenon, the Charities Publication Committee in the steel city of Pittsburgh commissioned a social study in 1907, the *Pittsburgh Survey*. Joseph Stella was commissioned to create illustrations [28] for this report. He produced about a hundred drawings of steelworkers (especially immigrants). About one-third of these illustrations were published in the journal *Charities and the Commons*.

			1918
1908 gyro compass	1911 F. W. Taylor: "Scientific Management"	1912 sinking of the Titanic	1913 coal liquification
	1914 - 1918 World War I		

World War I was the first large-scale industrial technological war with tremendous battles of material. Finally industry proved to be the basis of power – and not only the source of the improved standard of living for the nation. The years after 1918, particularly in Europe, were not only a time of political change but also of a complete restructuring of the economy, triggered by the war experience and the resulting economic challenges.

These changes also caused considerable labor confrontation. During this emotionally charged era, the creativity of art and culture flourished. "Work" was a subject of artistic production in many ways as never before. It was part of the political debate. The "classical" industrial painting was still being produced in great numbers, extolling technical accomplishments.

[30] Birkle, Albert: Worker and Machine, 1922

To this group belongs the painting of Fritz Jacobsen [29] painted for the *Deutsche Museum* in Munich, Germany. He depicts a new electric steel mill trying to combine technological accuracy with an expression of the factory atmosphere. In 1922 Albert Birkle, only 18 years old, painted works and machinery at the Borsig Company in Berlin [30]. Like other contemporaries, he represents the thesis of the worker's exploitation by the industrialist with the assistance of machinery.

[29] Jacobsen, Fritz: New Electric Steel Mill With Tippable Ovens, 1926

1918

Great Productivity Movement in Industry ⇨ implementation of the theories of Taylor, Ford, Industrial Engineering and Labor Psychology 1919 sound movies   1921 five millionth Henry Ford automobile   1923 passenger car diesel automobile

New forms of expression were sought in these years, stressing the rational and technical aspects of the subject matter, while criticizing the industrial working conditions. Charles Demuth [31] with Charles Sheeler and others in the USA, developed a constructionist presentation of industrial architecture. Modern industry was interpreted as a product of human rationality resulting in a new technical aesthetic. The title *My Egypt* compares the new factories with the pyramids of Egypt.

The 1920s in Germany were characterized by paintings and graphics critical of society. Many art associations were created to find and explore new visual analyses of society and the economy. By 1919 the *Group of Progressive Artists* was already founded in Cologne – also called *Political Constructionists*. Their theoretical leader was Franz Wilhelm Seiwert [32] with Gerd Arntz [2] as an influential member. Seiwert attempted to portray society's laws in the most simple and obnoxious way in order to influence changes in the society.

[31] Demuth, Charles: My Egypt, 1927

[32] Seiwert, Franz Wilhelm: Factory Organization, 1920

1924			1929
strong concentration (consolidation) of industry	1926 first demonstration of TV	1927 synthetic rubber	
	1928 plexiglass	1928/29 rocket experiments	

In the 1930s the political developments gathered momentum. Left wing artists contributed to social discourse with a huge number of paintings and graphics. Especially in the USA, a distinctly socialistic culture of art evolved. "The Black Graphic of the Red Decade" [33] was published in various journals, such as *New Masses.*

In Germany after 1933, the conventional industrial picture did not need to change much. It simply shifted in the direction of an increasing cult of power. Critical and progressive art was outlawed.

Work pictures of the '30s can be viewed as "Labor-Nationalism," and can be found in many European countries as well as in the USA. Often supported by government programs, the artists extolled the productivity and special quality of the national workforce as a response to economic depression. The aim was to improve the national self-esteem through highlighting the efficiency and productivity of its workforce. Thus, the individual countries were treated like private enterprises due to their involvement in global competition.

Especially in the USA, people began to re-examine their own history, expressed in success stories and works of art, particularly as huge wall murals. In the graphics there are many examples of the dominance of American work [34]. Famous examples for murals are the *America-Today* series by Thomas Hart Benton [35], and the Ford-Frescos in Detroit by Diego Rivera. The *Federal Art Project* of the *Works Progress Administration* supported 5,000 artists who produced 2,500 wall paintings, 17,000 sculptures, 108,000 paintings and 11,000 graphics. Many of these have a work theme as their focus.

In the 1930s and also in the war years, the illustration of work was openly used for political

[33] Karlin, Eugène: Night Shift, ca. 1938

[34] Levit, Herschel: Take it Away!, 1940

1929

Great Depression 1929 - 1932 ism	worldwide depression: 30 - 45 percent unemployment	age of labor national-
	1932 - 1939 "New Deal" with extensive work creation initiatives (make work)	

purposes. This was particularly true in the Soviet Union, Germany and the United States. In Great Britain the so-called *War Artists* were financed by the government for propaganda purposes. Famous artists such as Henry Moore, David Sutherland and Stanley Spencer created famous works during that time on the subject of work.

© AXA Financial, Inc.

[35] Benton, Thomas Hart: Steel from *America Today*, 1930, Distemper and egg tempera on gessoed linen with oil glaze, 92×117 in.

1935		1945
1933 - 1945 National Socialism in Germany	1938 synthetic perlon and nylon fibers	1939 first flight of a jet propelled aircraft (Hans von Ohain)
	1942 long range rockets	1939 - 1945 World War II	1945 atomic bomb

Even after World War II many artists continued to deal with the work theme. However, in the western nations the subject no longer captured the public interest because it was so heavily misused in the preceding years. In the arts, interest moved beyond the representations of objective art in favor of abstract and formalistic art.

However, there was a group of artists who stayed with the subject. An example is the prominent Fernand Léger with his large (2x3 meters) late work *The Constructors* [36] in which workers appear to build a technical world. The blue sky symbolizes hope

and harmony as well as perfect cooperation. However, the technology deforms nature and forces it to retreat. The clouds have an artificial appearance, and there is a severed tree branch with fruitless sprouts.

At the end of the 1960s, Roy Lichtenstein took up the subject of work in the Pop Art style [37]. He reflects the relationship of art and industry with simple means but with complex substance. From one point of view, he represents both art and industry in sharp contrast. One diagonal cut separates both segments of society. He clearly distinguishes these two spheres of society. Industry is maintained in cold blue

[36] Léger, Fernand: The Constructors, 1950

[37] Lichtenstein, Roy: Chemistry (Art and Industry), 1969

1945

1946 electronic mainframe computers (ENIAC)   1948 transistor   1951/52 hydrogen bomb
                                             1956 first nuclear power plant (England)   1957 first satellite (Sputnik)

while the art segment is expressed in warm colors. One side of the painting illustrates an airplane and a gear, while the other side presents birds and a flower. From another point of view, both segments become unified. The complementary colors not only symbolize contrast but also unity, and the overall presentation is done with formal methods that arise from the modern industrial and consumer society. In spite of all their differences, one cannot exist without the other. In the end, industry dominates.

As in all socialistic countries, human effort occupied a valued position in the former GDR or East Germany. Paintings and sculptures of work were promoted by the government [38]. In their official ideology, the socialistic states think of themselves as liberators and advocates of the working class. In innumerable works of art the "Heroes of Work" are celebrated along with the technical and organizational efforts of socialism. Here again, pictures of work have an expressed political function. In this regard they are intended to promote the consensus and legitimacy of the political order.

In West Germany Richard Gessner is still a leading industry painter. Post 1945, he discovered abstract forms with which to understand industrial landscapes [39]. His objective is to transmit an overall impression of the Ruhr industrial area.

[38] Cremer, Fritz: Recovery Helper, 1953

[39] Gessner, Richard: Industry at the Low Rhine, 1954

1960			1970
1960 laser 1961 first manned space flight	1961 first databank (storage system)		1969 moon landing

Work, as illustrated at the present time, can only be briefly considered. Examining only the more conventional nonabstract style of painting, one can see that the artists are focusing industry in a narrow sense, omitting all other kinds of work. Rarely are the subjects of crafts, agriculture, household work or the whole service sector chosen as subjects. Also, pictures of unemployment or working-class movements are rarely found. Views of industrial plants are dominant.

Hans Dieter Tylle belongs to a small circle of German artists who deal mainly with the subject of industry. With his *Steelworker* [40] he succeeds in producing a work of extraordinary impact. Another

[40] Tylle, Hans Dieter: Steelworker, Salzgitter, 1997

[41] Calvelli, Alexander: Blast Furnace at Thyssen Plant, 1995

1970

1972 microprocessor   1974 pocket calculator   1977 neutron bomb   1981 first IBM-PC   1982 Pershing II

[42] Hurwitz, Sidney: Bethlehem VI, 1997

Schneider [43] created extensive series of paintings of industries in East Germany (Bitterfeld), Poland (Slask, Silesia) and Aserbaidschan (Baku). His works can be understood as allegories of the twilight of a century.

Artists reluctantly commit to the new industries. It seems to be more difficult to paint modern nonmanual work. Many of the production processes are invisible or even "virtual" today. Modern art will need to develop new styles and forms in relation to the new forms of industry and work conditions.

important artist is Alexander Calvelli, who created hundreds of paintings both of old and new industries. He paints with outstanding accuracy, sometimes in a hyperrealistic manner. Therefore he is able to clearly represent the main structures of the industry plants, which can be seen in [41].

In the middle of the 1980s a new subject of industrial painting developed. A growing number of artists had been dealing with the downfall of old heavy industries, which had been a leading sector of the modern industrial societies. Blast furnaces and steel mills had served for more than a hundred years as symbols of the power of humanity over nature, as well as progress and wealth. Now the old giant facilities are presented as metaphors of the modern mode of production, of which the basic principles are cycles of utilization and devaluation.

Artists like Sidney Hurwitz in the USA and Robert Schneider in Germany developed an "Aesthetics of Decline." Hurwitz finds a common source in the huge complex of Bethlehem-Steel [42].

2002

1989/90 collapse of socialistic states in Europe

[43] Schneider, Robert: Śląsk Nr. 35, 1995

For Further Reading:

Brandt, Paul: *Schaffende Arbeit und bildende Kunst.* 2 volumes, Leipzig 1927/28.

Klingender, Francis D.: *Art and The Industrial Revolution.* London 1947.

Lucie-Smith, Edward/Dars, Celestine: *Work and Struggle. The Painter as Witness 1870-1914.* New York and London 1977.

Smithsonian Institution (ed.): *The Working American.* Exhibition Catalogue. New York 1979.

Fazio, Beverly (ed.): T*he Machine Age in America.* Exhibition Catalogue. New York 1986.

Donegan, Rosemary: *Industrial Images.* Exhibition Catalogue. Hamilton, Ontario 1988.

Royot, Daniel/Goldberg, Itzhak/Lebard, Daniel: *L`Amérique de la Dépression. Artistes engagés des années 30.* Exhibition Catalogue. Paris 1996.

Mainz, Valerie/Pollock, Griselda (eds.): *Work, Craft and Labour. Visual Representations in Changing Histories. Work and Image I.* Aldershot 2000.

Mainz, Valerie/Pollock, Griselda (eds.): *Work in Modern Times. Visual Mediations and Social Processes. Work and Image II.* Aldershot 2000.

Dabakis, Melissa: *Visualizing Labor in American Sculpture. Monuments, Manliness, and the Work Ethic, 1880-1935.* Cambridge 1999.

Türk, Klaus: *Bilder der Arbeit. Eine ikonografische Anthologie.* Wiesbaden 2000. [You will find there about 1,500 reproductions of artworks and more than a thousand further references.]

Credits:

1: Stichting Vrienden van het werk van de industrieschilder Herman Heijenbrock, Amsterdam

18: Musée de l'Art wallon de la Ville de Liège

19: Museum of Fine Arts Boston; Gift of Quincy Adams Shaw through Quincy Adam Shaw, Jr., and Mrs. Marian Shaw Haughton; 17.1485

20: museum kunst palast, Düsseldorf

22: Ecomusée de la Communauté Urbaine Le Creusot Montceau-Les-Mindes, Cliché Daniel Busseuil

23: Staatliche Museen zu Berlin – Preußischer Kulturbesitz, Nationalgalerie

24: Fine Arts Museums of San Francisco, Museum purchase, Gift of Mr. and Mrs. John D. Rockefeller 3rd, 1979.7.4

25: Deutsches Historisches Museum, Berlin

26: Historisches Archiv Krupp, Essen

27: Musée des Beaux-Arts de Rennes

28: Carnegie Library of Pittsburgh

29: Deutsches Museum, München

30: Collection Josef Hierling, Tutzing

31: Whitney Museum of American Art, New York; purchase, with funds from Gertrude Vanderbilt Whitney 31.172

33, 34: Collection Daniel Lebard, Paris

35: Collection, AXA Financial, Inc., through its subsidiary The Equitable Life Insurance Society of the U.S.

36: Musée National Fernand Léger, Biot; © VG Bild-Kunst, Bonn 2003

37: Städtisches Museum Schloss Salder, Salzgitter; © VG Bild-Kunst, Bonn 2003

38: Photo: Niklas Türk, Berlin

39: Sigrun Gessner, Düsseldorf

40: Hans Dieter Tylle, Kassel

41: Alexander Calvelli, Köln

42: Sidney Hurwitz, Boston

43: Robert Schneider, Hamburg; © VG Bild-Kunst, Bonn 2003

All other photographs: Archive of the author

THE ECKHART G. GROHMANN COLLECTION

The ECKHART G. GROHMANN COLLECTION, with more than 450 works of art, covers a time span of more than 400 years. The majority of the collection consists of oil paintings supplemented by a large variety of bronze sculptures. The collection is primarily focused on an historical presentation of production technologies and individual work processes. The overall goal of the collection is not necessarily to represent the highest artistic achievement but rather to collect and present visual documentation of the related histories of culture, work and technology. Nevertheless, the collection contains many outstanding examples of European art including works by Brueghel, Valckenborch, van Goyen and Liebermann.

A large portion of the paintings and bronzes deals with the theme of metalworking, especially the subject of iron and steel processing. This is explained by the particular interests of the collector and also by this subject's dominance of the historical images of work and industry. Over the ages many myths and fables have evolved around the forming of metal. The industrial age is distinctively influenced by this sector particularly because metalworking innovation created military and economic success.

Of special appeal to the art world are those activities that utilize and transform natural raw materials into useful objects. In addition to the mining and processing of metals, the whole sector of textile production plays a great role in the history of culture and art. It is well represented in the collection with several important works. An outstanding example is the composition oil study by Max Liebermann leading to his world renowned *Flax Barn at Laren*.

A third important sector of productive work is construction and building, including the mining of natural materials, particularly the quarrying of stone. Images from this trade are found from early antiquity.

While these three sectors form the core of the ECKHART G. GROHMANN COLLECTION, they cannot cover the entire spectrum of human work. But with respect to the historical process of industrialization, these three sectors can be considered thoroughly representative. Additionally, the collection includes a great number of paintings and sculptures depicting other work activities and offers the student a comprehensive presentation of the range of human work.

The collection is housed at *Milwaukee School of Engineering* in Milwaukee, Wis. The university was founded in 1903 and is world renowned for its applications-oriented approach to education. Today, the university offers 16 undergraduate and six graduate programs for its more than 2,600 hundred students from 26 countries.

1. Mining and Metals

Introductory Comments On Iron Production

In its natural state, iron is almost never found in pure form but only in the oxidized form or in combination with other metals. Upon heating iron ore with coal (charcoal, hard coal) to a temperature of 932 °F, the oxygen is driven off. Because the melting point of iron is a rather high 2796.8 °F, the common impurities melt away at lower temperatures, generally by 2012 °F. Up to the 14th century, the temperature required to melt iron had not been achieved. Thus the iron was softened sufficiently to be forged but did not achieve the temperature and fluidity to allow casting in a mold. In addition, this early iron contained very little carbon and hence was relatively soft. A carbon content of 0.6 percent to 2 percent is required to produce what we know as steel or even hard iron. Hardening the iron by forging or by the addition of carbon by various processes employing water, oil or oxblood, was considered an "industrial secret" for many years to come.

All this changed with the 14th century development of the blast furnace, which drove air through the coal fire to increase the temperature. Now it became possible to pour iron. However, in contrast to the older smelting ovens, the iron now absorbed more carbon than desired, destroying its forging properties. The solution was to burn off some of the carbon in a refining fire.

In the early 18th century, hard coal replaced charcoal in the iron smelting process. But even the hard coal had impurities that could spoil the iron. Thus the coal was purified by heating (called coking), producing coke. The first iron smelter employing hard coal appeared in Coalbrookdale, England, in 1735.

With the passage of time, several additional smelting processes were developed to improve the quality of iron. The most significant of these, also illustrated in the ECKHART G. GROHMANN COLLECTION, are:

• **Crucible steel**

Developed in 1740 by Benjamin Huntsman to melt steels of diverse compositions in a specially lined crucible to produce homogenous steel.

• **Puddle process**

A drawback of the use of hard coal was the contact between coal and iron, allowing the sulphur content of the coal to find its way into the iron, leading to negative properties. The puddling process (developed by Henry Cort in 1783) allows only the flame (and not the coal) to impinge upon the iron. The oxidizing effect of the gas flame is aided by puddling, or stirring, which repeatedly exposes the slag and the iron to the air to oxidize the impurities. The slag is then removed by rolling and the result is forgeable iron.

• **Bessemer process**

Puddle furnaces did not have sufficient capacity or quality to satisfy the increased demand for iron and steel. An Englishman, Henry Bessemer, developed a process of blowing air through molten iron in a crucible. This greatly increased the exposure of the iron to air and accelerated the oxidation of the impurities to slag. Thus, an iron batch that required 24 hours in a conventional puddling furnace would be treated in 20 minutes in the Bessemer process. One drawback to Bessemer's technique was the insufficient removal of phosphorus from the iron.

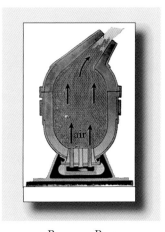

Bessemer Pear

• **Thomas process**

By lining the *Bessemer Pear* (the crucible, so named because of its shape) with an alkaline material, the problem phosphorus was removed from the iron melt. In modern terminology, both the *Bessemer* and *Thomas crucibles* are called "converters."

• **Siemens-Martin process**

In order to handle larger batches of crude iron and to add recycled scrap steel, the Siemens-Martin (or "open-hearth") process was developed. The gas-fired process takes place in an open pit with air blown through the iron melt.

The ECKHART G. GROHMANN COLLECTION contains many paintings depicting blast furnaces. The most important parts of the blast furnace are illustrated in the schematic drawing below. The vertical blast furnace tube is charged at the top with iron ore, coke, limestone and other additives. To obtain the required temperature, preheated air is blown into the bottom of the blast furnace, sometimes with additional fuel. The charge moves downward through the furnace as the heated air moves upward. The burning of the coke produces carbon monoxide, which reduces the iron oxide to iron in a molten state. In modern blast furnaces the hot gases are captured at the top of the furnace and used to preheat the air entering the furnace. In more primitive cases the air is not heated but simply blown cold into the base of the blast furnace. The liquid iron gathers at the bottom of the blast furnace and is tapped out. Slag is also removed and used as a byproduct, for example, in road construction and building materials. Part of the slag is formed by limestone introduced to absorb the sulphur content of the coke. Finally, the iron may be carbon enriched and thus form steel. The complete detail of steel production is much more complex than described here, but this description will suffice to understand the paintings on this subject in the ECKHART G. GROHMANN COLLECTION at the *Milwaukee School of Engineering*.

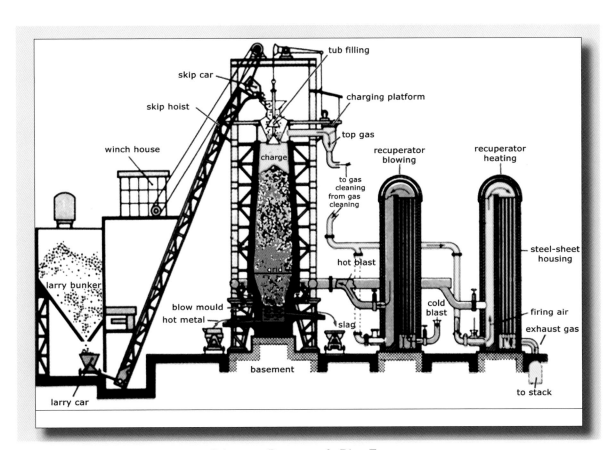

Schematic Drawing of a Blast Furnace

1.1 PREINDUSTRIAL METALWORKING SCENES

The Mythology of Forging

For centuries, European mythology attributed a great deal of mystery to the forging of iron. Understanding the process was rudimentary with the knowledge gaps filled with nontechnical inputs. The process of shaping and hardening iron, resulting in the creation of powerful weaponry as well as artistically crafted objects, was always considered admirable and a highly esteemed skill. Controlling and then utilizing the often horrendously destructive fire for productive purposes made the blacksmith appear in concert with both heavenly and devilish powers. The heat and the whooshing and howling noise of the bellows provided an extra-worldly atmosphere. The resulting myths and stories are based simultaneously on fear, superstition and admiration.

Hephaistos, the crippled son of Zeus and Hera, is the God of Fire, thus the God of the blacksmith shop and the metalworking tradespeople. In Greek mythology, Hephaistos, together with the one-eyed Cyclops, creates lightning. In Roman mythology Hephaistos loses his place to Vulcan as the God of Fire and the forger of weapons. Vulcan also serves as the forger of Amor's love arrows. Vulcan is married to the beautiful Goddess Venus who is ultimately unfaithful to him with the God of War, Mars.

The Old Testament considers Tubalcain, a descendant of Cain, to be the first blacksmith and also the inventor of music. The Germanic forger of artwork, Wieland, is imprisoned because of his artistic skills and condemned to hard labor. His knees are broken to prevent him from escaping. However, he still manages to escape with self-constructed wings.

Because very few understood metalworking, and then in only a basic manner, such myths and fables found their way into the fine arts description of these processes. Over a period of 2,000 years, and even to the middle of the 20th century, countless paintings and sculptures were created of the blacksmith at work. All express admiration for the subject. During the 19th and 20th centuries the blacksmith leaves the context of Greek and Roman mythology to present himself as the symbol of power, productivity and maker of weapons. In ancient art we find him often in both more differentiated and exciting presentations.

Central to this mythological view of metalworking is the visit of Venus to Vulcan's forge, whereby she wants to persuade him to produce weapons for her lover, Mars.

Boet, Johan Hans [Dutch, 17th century]: Venus and Cupid in the Forge of Vulcan, oil on copper mounted on panel, 14.5 × 18.5 in., 1659 (after Jan Brueghel), private collection Dr. Grohmann

In this context we find the typical figure, the God of Love, or Cupid, accompanies Venus. Additional forging stations (usually three), referring to Cyclops, are seen doing her work. This grouping indicates the human existence as a unity of contradictions: male and female, ugliness and beauty, war and love, reason and feeling, work and art.

The most intensive and impressive treatment of this subject was done by Jan Brueghel the Elder. At least nine oil paintings are known to have been created together with figure painter Henrik van Balen. However, one cannot be absolutely sure whether one painting or another might not be the work of Jan Brueghel the Younger. This is the case with the illustrated Brueghel painting from the ECKHART G. GROHMANN COLLECTION, which could be a copy by the Younger of one of his father's work. A second work in the ECKHART G. GROHMANN COLLECTION was created by Johan Hans Boet after a painting by Jan Brueghel the Elder. It represents in essential detail Brueghel's *Allegory of Fire* created in 1611.

Not only has Brueghel repeated his paintings in different presentations, he also selected various details from existing works to compose different new paintings. Thus we find individual groupings from these ECKHART G. GROHMANN COLLECTION paintings by Brueghel and Van Balen, and in other paintings as well. The work-pieces in the foreground – all military armor of the 16th century – are taken from the major work *Allegory of Fire.* The scene in the middle of the painting is repeated again as

Brueghel, Jan I: Mars Receives his Weapons, 1613

a separate work entitled *Mars Receives His Weapons* in 1613, and the right side detail was used again in an additional, separate oil painting in 1623 by Brueghel and Van Balen.

As in all of Brueghel's paintings dealing with Vulcan's forge, the total scene is placed within a Roman ruin landscape. The historical origin of the myth is illustrated,

as well as its end. The history is good only for allegories. In the left background of *Vulcan in Mars Receives His Weapons,* you see a volcano spewing fire, as in other pictures (for example, von Boet in the ECKHART G. GROHMANN COLLECTION). The blacksmith workers are placed in the right background, almost underground and behind the pulled back curtain. The secret, and thus mysterious, act of processing iron is briefly open to the viewer. Vulcan shows Venus a shield, which she examines (*Venus at the Forge of Vulcan*). The shield bears the crest of the Duke of Savoyen, who probably commissioned this artwork. The precious oriental carpet and the white-breasted dogs depict the taste and fashion of the time. The chandelier with burned-out candles symbolizes a typical manneristic element.

Overall this painting again symbolizes contrasting elements; the beauty of Venus versus the dark ugliness of the forge, and especially the production of war material contrasted with the beautiful art objects at the right side of the painting. But both war and luxury are attributes of the aristocratic ruling elite for whom Vulcan is working, as well as for Venus, his wife. Venus appears to be part of this elite society and apparently the noble art patron should identify with her and the affluence and luxury attributed to her in the painting.

Brueghel, Jan I/Hendrik van Balen: Venus at the Forge of Vulcan, 1623

Brueghel, Jan II [Dutch, 1601-1678]/Balen, Hendrik van [Flemish, 1575-1632]: Venus at the Forge of Vulcan, oil on panel, 21×34 in., ca. 1613-1627, monogrammed "HHBA 16[.]7 DEN 3[?] JULIUS"

Early Paintings of Furnaces

Some years before Brueghel, the Belgian brothers Lucas and Marten Valckenborch created landscape paintings depicting iron ore mining and ore processing. The ECKHART G. GROHMANN COLLECTION includes two of the most beautiful as well as complete works of this subject, the oil painting *A River Landscape With Iron Smelter*, painted around 1600, and *Phantastic River Landscape with Ironworks* of 1609, both painted by Marten.

However, the Valckenborch brothers were not the first artists to paint iron ore processing using a blast furnace. About 60 years earlier an unknown painter, Herri met de Bles, from the Dutch School of Joachim Patenier painted *Landscape with Ironworks*. As in the painting by Valckenborch, Herri met de Bles illustrates a scene in the Belgian Mense Valley near the town of Luettich. Beyond the river are iron mines as well as lime kilns. On the near side of the river we see the entire process of iron production with blast furnace, reheat fire and forge hammer. Workers deliver iron ore, charge the blast furnace with the ore and charcoal, tap the blast furnace to allow the molten iron to flow into ingot molds, stack the iron ingots, maintain the fire (left, next to the blast furnace) and knock off the scale under the forge hammer. At the lower right in the picture you find another blast furnace. A water wheel drives the bellows and the forge hammer.

Herri met de Bles produced five known versions of his *Landscape with Ironworks*. The version pictured here describes the iron production in extraordinary detail. At right the iron ore is mined and broken into small pieces. Left of center it is being washed to remove soil and other impurities. Mixed with charcoal and other additives, the ore is charged into the blast furnace shown in the middle of the picture. The ingots, initially poured into sand, are broken into component pieces and exposed to the heat of the fire to remove the excessive surface carbon. In the forge shop on the far left, the excess scale is hammered off and the ironwork is hardened. In an attempt to attract attention and interest to the overall industrial scene, a story from the Bible is depicted: in the left foreground, Herri met de Bles illustrates the flight of the Holy Family to Egypt.

In most paintings by the brothers Valckenborch, ore mines and ironworks are rather incidentally added to a fantastic landscape. The Valckenborch paintings in the ECKHART G. GROHMANN COLLECTION are entirely different. Here the processing of the iron ore is the main subject, while the landscape, although grand, merely provides the background. Standing on a hill, the viewer sees the blast furnace in the foreground or center respectively being charged by a worker. At the bottom of

Herri met de Bles: Landscape With Ironworks and the Flight to Egypt, ca. 1540

the blast furnace, iron runs into a sand mold.

The design of the blast furnace is identical to that of the first successful furnace built in America, near Boston, Mass., in 1645. This design, shown in the figure below, employed a rotary source to power the bellows to drive air into the blast furnace. The bellows for the Valckenborch blast furnaces are driven by a water wheel power source. This design was typical of American blast furnaces for another 200 years.

The forge hammer in the middle of the background in the 1600 painting (to the left in the 1609 painting) is powered by turning water wheels. In the forge shop to the right of the anvil burns a purifying fire used to decarburize the iron for the forging process. In both pictures two workers bring newly produced iron to the shop. The iron ore is mined above the forge shops on the hill slope. In the 1600 painting, lime apparently is mined on the opposite side of the river and transported by boat to the blast furnace.

Almost all Valckenborch paintings of the iron and steel industry use a special event to create a painting of an industrial process. For example, the Valckenborchs always use passersby, such as hikers or robbers. In the 1600 painting, the shepherd to the left has a particular role to play. He drives his flock of sheep and accidentally appears to find the iron ore plant. The goat in the left corner could be a space-filling addition, but it also may have a hidden symbolic meaning.

There are some significant differences between the two paintings. The later of the two, *Phantastic River Landscape with Ironworks*, is not only of larger scale but divided by the river into two distinct areas. The left half depicts the iron industry while the right illustrates farming. Thus the traditional and newly evolved forms of work are divided and yet bound together in a new whole, one that is not yet totally merged into a single new entity. The result is a work of great symbolic meaning at the dawn of the modern society.

From: *The Making, Shaping and Treating of Steel*, McGannon, H.E. (Ed.) Ninth Edition, United States Steel Corp., 1971.

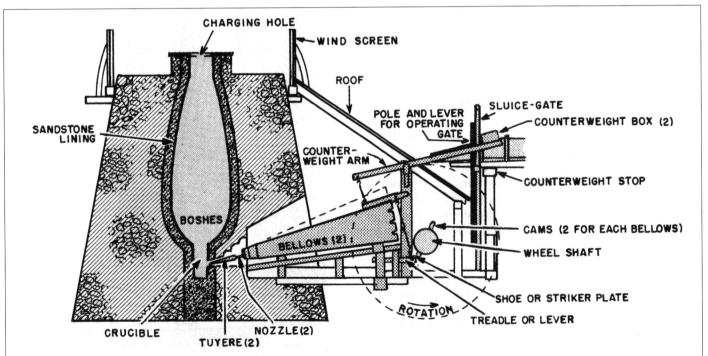

FIG. 1—6. Schematic cross-section of the Hammersmith furnace near Saugus, Massachusetts, restored by the American Iron and Steel Institute. Water from the sluice turned the overshot water wheel. Cams on the axle of the wheel engaged the treadle or lever and exerted a squeezing force on the bellows that compressed the air for the blast. The raw materials were dumped into the charge hole at the top of the stack, and molten iron was run from the furnace through an opening in the wall of the crucible. This opening was near the bottom of the crucible on the side facing the reader, and was kept plugged except when molten iron was run.

Valckenborch, Marten van
[Flemish, 1535-1612]: A River
Valley With Iron Smelter, oil
on canvas, 29×45 in., ca. 1600,
monogrammed "M/VV"

Valckenborch, Marten
van [Flemish, 1535-
1612]: Phantastic
River Landscape
With Ironworks, oil
on canvas, 38×65.5 in.,
1609, monogrammed
"M/VV/FECIT/A
1609/AET 74"

The Romanticism of Forges

Bürkel, Heinrich [German, 1802-1869]: Forge in Winter, oil on canvas, 23×36 in., ca. 1860, signed

During the first half of the 19th century, a new cultural trend toward romanticism developed in Europe as a reaction to rationalism and industrialism. Romanticism stresses the close relationship between man and nature. The two paintings illustrated here by Heinrich Bürkel and Richard Zimmerman are typical of the paintings in that category. Human labor appears closely tied to nature and dependent on nature. The human work adjusts modestly to the natural circumstances, thereby underlining a stronger dependence on nature than on industry.

Both blacksmith shops are placed on a mountain stream in order to utilize the power of the falling water to drive the bellows and the forge hammer. The artists chose the winter season to emphasize the dependence on nature. The streams can freeze and subsequently interrupt the operation of the forge. Yet the scenic winter landscape also romantically depicts the idyllic loneliness of the subject. Both pictures belong to the painting genre dealing with stories of everyday lives.

Zimmerman, Richard [German, 1820-1875]: Forge on
the Mountain, oil on canvas, 32×39.5 in., signed

Blacksmiths at Their Forges

Beelt, Cornelis [Dutch, 1640 ?-1702]: Inside a Forge, oil on panel, 17×21.5 in.

The painting of genre subjects was especially popular in the Netherlands during the 17th century. The first three paintings in this chapter belong in that category. Cornelis Beelt paints a master blacksmith along with a journeyman, apprentice, and a woman. The apprentice apparently is learning how to forge hot workpieces on the anvil within a team of three, swinging the hammer in rhythmic order. The journeyman at the right, whose position is temporarily occupied by the apprentice, takes a break for a quick smoke. Interiors and individuals are shown as they probably existed at the time, contradicting the idealistic tradition of the blacksmith painting. However, it is typical

**Anonymous [Dutch, 17th c.]: The Forge, oil on panel,
11×19 in.**

for the Dutch realism of that time. In the same manner we find the oil painting above by an anonymous painter, in which the realistic condition of the forge shop is even more apparent. The two working blacksmiths are old and worn. The third man in the center appears weak and tired and enhances his rest with a bit of tobacco. These paintings are created about one generation after the Vulcan paintings by Brueghel and appear to be critical opposites. Reality is contrasted to myth.

Lundens, Gerrit [Dutch, 1622-1677]: At the Forge, oil
on panel, 20×16 in., 1655, signed

Although placed in a work environment, no work is being performed here. Friends and relatives, children and adults, have gathered in the blacksmith shop, perhaps to warm up from unpleasant weather outside. Fire and smoke are created largely by the men's enjoyment of tobacco. The anvil serves as a seat rather than a tool. The man standing in front of the forge, turning toward the view, seems to hold a tobacco pouch in his right hand. The new fashion of smoking as a leisure social activity and a respite from labor seems to be the theme of the painting.

**Kotulla, Dominik [Bohemian, *1795]: Coppersmith
Reading a Letter, oil on panel, 15×12.5 in.**

The original title of the Kotulla painting in the ECKHART
G. GROHMANN COLLECTION is unknown. It represents a
typical genre scene in which a story is told. The coppersmith interrupts his work in order to read a letter brought
to him in his workshop by his wife, and his wonderful
wares are in full view. His wife has obviously already read
the letter. The somewhat nearsighted older man is fascinated by it while the woman looks on smiling. The letter
probably contains good news, perhaps from one of their
children.

Jacque, Charles Emile [French, 1813-1894]: Blacksmith at the Forge, etching, 3×2 in., 1843, signed

Jacque, Charles Emile [French, 1813-1894]: Blacksmith at the Forge, etching, 6×5 in., 1850, signed

In the middle of 19th century France, a new direction in art developed, focusing on the reality of the common workers. The most famous example is Jean-François Millet, who devoted his effort almost exclusively to farmhands and farmers. Charles Emile Jacque was well acquainted with him and shared his artistic objectives. The etchings and the oil painting pictured on these pages distinctly show his artistic proximity to Millet.

In contrast to the genre painters, the aim is not to show harmony and beauty but rather to recognize the situation confronting this hard-working class. Jacque's blacksmith toils hard in a dark workshop to earn his daily bread. The 1843 etching reveals to the viewer the difficult life that his family leads, even though they are not at the bottom of the economic ladder.

With his bowed back – a symbol of exhausting manual work often found in the history of work in art – the blacksmith labors in his workplace. There are no reminders of the myths of Vulcan. Hardly noticeable, to the right in the painting, a second man labors at the anvil, totally blending into the dark work surroundings without any signs of individuality.

Jacque, Charles Emile [French, 1813-1894]: Blacksmith at His Forge, oil on canvas, 20×10 in.

Schendel, Petrus van [1806-1870]: The Blacksmith's
Forge, oil on panel, 19.5×24 in.

Eight blacksmiths are at work in a large blacksmith shop. Three fires are available to heat the iron. In the middle stands an anvil surrounded by the blacksmiths. This appears to be an early shop with multiple workers and an early depiction of a division of labor. Common laborers, rather than skilled blacksmiths, heat the workpieces. The blacksmiths are focused only on the skilled forging process at the anvil. No daylight penetrates the shop; all light originates from fire and glowing iron.

Riefenstahl, Robert [1823-1903]: In the Forge Barn, oil on canvas, 16×21 in., signed

This painting probably dates from the same period as the one shown to the left. This shop is equipped with a hammer mounted on a wood beam, driven by water power (left) and activated by a pull mechanism. In the middle, four workers are apparently removing a large workpiece from the oven. It still glows brightly and is moved toward the forge hammer.

Carolus, Jean [Belgian, 19th c.]: A Busy Wheelwright Forge Shop, oil on panel, 21.5×28.5 in., ca. 1870, signed

Frère, Charles Edouard [French, 1837-1894]: The Wheelwright's Forge, oil on canvas, 22×32 in., 1878, signed

For a thousand years, wagons have used wooden wheels. Fitting wooden wheels with a steel rim strengthens the wheel and extends its life. Like a horseshoe, the rim must fit perfectly on the wheel perimeter. When wheels were individual products of a wheelwright, every wheel rim had to be fitted individually. These three paintings in the ECK-

**Lippmann, Johannes [German]: Six Workers in a Wheelwright's
Forge, oil on canvas cardboard, 31.5×23.5 in., 1922, signed**

HART G. GROHMANN COLLECTION show three developmental steps of the wheelwright's forge. The first painting shows a small workshop in a domestic setting. The second painting shows forge work in a different setting, already expanded to several workers. Finally, the third painting presents a view of an early manufacturer with a division of labor. In each case, a hot and somewhat pliable rim is fitted onto the wooden wheel. After cooling and contracting, the steel rim fits tightly around the wheel and it can carry heavier loads.

This blacksmith produces rims for wagon wheels. The center blacksmith employs an unusually heavy forging hammer, while the worker at the fire is heating or reheating a work piece. A bellows with a large pipe blows air into the fire to increase the temperature.

Anonymous: Forge, oil on canvas, 23×28.5 in.

In a village blacksmith shop, the master works with a journeyman and an apprentice. His helpers work the bellows for the fire while he watches his workpiece heat to the correct temperature. Two anvils stand ready to forge the workpiece into the desired shape and harden it.

Firmin-Girard, Marie François [French, 1838-1921]: At the Blacksmith's Shop, oil on canvas, 28×39 in., signed

McGregor, Robert [Scottish, 1848-1922]: Village Blacksmith, oil on canvas, 16×19.5 in., signed

A bearded blacksmith is working on a red-glowing horseshoe. He seems to be explaining the process to his journeyman. On the shop floor lie several horseshoes that appear to be of poor quality. Perhaps the journeyman has produced some unacceptable products. Both wear typical aprons made of heavy leather to shield them from the heat and flying sparks.

Kern, Hermann [Hungarian, 1839-1912]: Blacksmith,
oil on panel, 15×19 in., 1905, signed

Hermann Kern painted these three village blacksmith shops. Above, a farrier or horseshoe blacksmith, holds a horseshoe with his tongs in his right hand. With the left hand he controls his bellows. The blacksmith at the upper right increases the temperature of his fire by pumping the bellows. The blacksmith at lower right seems to be doing more detailed forming, working on a small tin can that he holds in his left hand with tongs. There seems to be a similarity among the figures, perhaps due to using the same model.

Kern, Hermann [Hungarian, 1839-1912]: Blacksmith,
oil on canvas, 24×28.5 in., 1906, signed

Kern, Hermann [Hungarian, 1839-1912]: Blacksmith,
oil on panel, 17×20 in., 1905, signed

Stoll, J. [Austrian]: Blacksmith, oil on canvas, 16×20 in., signed

The village blacksmith appears bemused. It is uncertain whether his state of mind is related to the large number of drinking vessels gathered around his workplace. The wooden pail in the left foreground contains water and serves to temper the forged workpieces. His main occupation seems to be the repair of wagons and carriages. To the right foreground is the front wheel of an open-framed wooden handcart. At the base of the anvil are several horseshoe slugs on their way to becoming horseshoes. Smaller tools and other devices are seen beside the basic tools such as the hammer and anvil. At the left, behind the blacksmith, is a heavy forged vise. His left hand operates the bellows, providing an air blast to the fire within the hearth and producing the heat necessary for forging.

Beauregard, Charles [American, 1856-1880]: The Blacksmith, oil on canvas, 16×20 in., ca. 1880, signed

Here again the subject is a horseshoe blacksmith, holding a horseshoe in the fire. He also fabricates wheel rims for wagon wheels, as indicated by the wheel in the background next to the window. A special hammer enabling the forge to create bowed shapes out of sheet metal lies on the anvil.

Vroen, Henry (?): Blacksmith With Large Hat, oil on canvas, 8×12 in., signed

This blacksmith forges a new tool out of iron. In his left hand he holds a large pair of tongs to form the workpiece, which he moves with his right hand. The painter depicts the smoke and flying sparks very artistically and decoratively, as shown in the detail to the right.

Kunz, V.: Blacksmith at Work, oil on canvas, 28×34 in., ca. 1900, signed

By blowing air into the fire, this blacksmith has elevated his fire to a high temperature. The fire is unusually large and gets the needed airflow from an electrically driven blower. In contrast to many earlier blacksmith portrayals, we see a somewhat younger man without the typical attribute of a beard. This workshop seems well organized and neat, indicating another break with the traditional blacksmith painting.

Ostersetzer, Carl C. [German]: The Blacksmith, oil on
cardboard, 18×12 in., signed

Here again we see an independent horseshoe blacksmith, working at his trade with simple tools to make a living for his family. The painter evokes sympathy for his subject, who is standing in the glow of his fire. His small hammer implies he is adding the final touches to his workpiece.

Schmidt, Edward Allan [English, 1825-1893]: The Armorer's Shop, oil on panel, 10×8 in., 1889, signed

This historical painting draws us back to the middle ages. An armorer is finishing a knight's suit of armor. The upper parts of the armor, consisting of helmet, breastplate and arm protection, are on his workbench. It appears he is finishing the wire frame for a component of a sheet metal suit, perhaps the elbow of the right arm. At the right corner we see a large engraved metal plate depicting a knight adored by several ladies.

Braekeleer, Adrien Ferdinand de [Belgian, 1818-1904]:
The Armor Shop, oil on panel, 25×32 in., 1851, signed

The two paintings on this double page illustrate a 16th or 17th century armorer's shop, from the perspective of a 19th century artist. The paintings are intended to be historical reminders of times past. The left picture relates to the Netherlands while the right focuses on Spain. The Netherlands fought an 80-year war of independence from Spain, from 1568 to 1648. Braekeleer composes a scene in which a gentleman and his associate critically examine a dagger forged for him by the master armorer, to the right. At the left, on the floor, is the breastplate of a suit of armor. In the background is the workshop.

Zamacois y Zabala, Eduardo [Spanish, 1842-1871]: A Visit to the Armor Shop, oil on canvas, 18×22 in., signed

In this Spanish version of armor production the armorer holds a newly fabricated piece on his lap as it is being thoroughly inspected by a customer. The soldier carries a heavy gun, and is wearing high leather boots and an impressive cloak over his shoulder. To the left lie two long spears with tips probably forged by the armorer. Both paintings are done in genre fashion and are intended to entertain the middle class of the 19th century.

**Montan, Anders [Swedish, 1846-1917]: The Broken
Coffee Grinder, oil on canvas, 26×30.5 in., signed**

Montan paints the varied interior of a blacksmith shop. A young woman has just arrived out of the rain in pursuit of an urgent matter – the coffee grinder doesn't work. The friendly master tries to assess the damage. For this problem his heavy tools may not be of much help. The apprentice, holding the rope for pumping the bellows in his left hand, watches with interest. The journeyman, on the other hand, is unimpressed and remains at the window continuing his work uninterrupted.

**Henckel, Karl [German, *1881]: Forge Shop in
Westphalia, Germany, oil on canvas, 17.5×14 in., signed**

The blacksmith has established his workshop in the entrance of a larger house. In addition to his normal activities, he also performs maintenance work, as indicated by his tools and vices. The master and journeyman work on the anvil while the apprentice keeps the fire at the correct temperature. Wheels for the steel rims that are being fabricated lie on the floor to the right and farther back. A large rim stands at the extreme right. The painter depicts two sources of light. Bright sunlight beams into the workshop from a window at the upper left, while a second light source is the blacksmith's fire.

Montan, Anders [Swedish, 1846-1917]: The Coppersmith, oil on canvas, 19×15.5 in., 1887, signed

A coppersmith is at work finishing a teakettle that is on his lap. Sunlight streams through the small window of his modest workshop providing him with light and perhaps a source of warmth. He wears a heavy leather apron, wooden shoes and a leather vest – the typical work clothes of his trade. On the floor to the left are various products including a pistol with copper trim. The special anvil in front of him is primarily used to form copper sheet into rounded shapes.

**Hölzel, Adolf [German, 1853-1934]: Peasant Kitchen
With Copper Ware, oil on canvas, 14.5×23 in.,
monogrammed "A H."**

Kitchen utensils produced by a coppersmith were commonly used in farming households. By the use of light and color, the painter guides the viewer through the interior of a farmer's kitchen to the right wall. A large variety of pots, pans and scoops hang on the wall, indicating a well appointed kitchen. In the center is a rough worktable in front of a cooking stove. A pot sits on the back of the stove. The cook has left the kitchen, perhaps to fetch food from the storage room to the right.

Krøyer, Peder Severin [Danish, 1851-1909]: Three Smiths at Hornbæk, Denmark, oil on canvas, 37×46 in., 1877, signed

This painting by the famous Danish artist Peder Severin Krøyer records the master blacksmith in the Danish town of Hornbæk. The master is working with a journeyman and an apprentice. Krøyer painted a slightly earlier version of this theme in 1875 (lower right). The master holds a large workpiece in his tongs. The impact of the hammer creates sparks as it produces the desired shape. The apprentice operates the bellows.

Fischer, H. [German]: Drop Forge, oil on canvas, 16×21 in., 1928, signed

From the Middle Ages until after World War II, water power was commonly employed to drive long-handled European forge hammers. A water wheel drives a cam shaft to lift the hammer and allow it to fall again. Large workpieces could be forged to considerable strength with this style of collar hammer at the end of a long, sturdy shaft. The noise and vibration were enormous. This painting by Fischer provides a good illustration of the wooden structure of the hammer facility and its capabilities.

Anonymous after Friedrich von Keller: Drop Forge, oil on canvas, 24×40 in., ca. 1900

Both sides of this double page show hammer forge shops. Friedrich von Keller painted a large number of forge and stone quarry pictures. An unknown artist admired these paintings and produced copies. As is clear in both paintings, working metal with large forge hammers requires well-practiced working teams. The workpieces were held with tongs, intermittently reheated in the fire and forged blow by blow under the hammer. In the left picture, an

Anonymous after Friedrich von Keller: Drop Forge, oil on canvas, 26×35.5 in., ca. 1900

additional worker observes the process with a critical eye. Family members are seen at the door in the background. In the oil sketch to the right, a large glowing steel block is forged by the water-powered hammer. The whole scene is given a romantic atmosphere by placing it in a grotto. The glowing workpiece dominates the picture but the harnessing of water power dominates the process.

Crowe, Eyre A.R.A. [British, 1824-1910]: The Forge, oil on canvas, 60×94 in., 1869, signed

The artist illustrates a forge shop featuring a drop forge hammer. A pair of workers position a hot workpiece under the forge hammer, their faces shielded from sparks and heat. The workpiece lies on an iron base serving as an anvil. A cam wheel to the right lifts the hammer. As the cam turns further the hammer will fall onto the hot glowing workpiece. The young man at the right operates a pushcart transporting workpieces throughout the shop. To the left of the painting, a worker takes a break and eats a meal served to him by a young woman.

This painting was part of the *Forbes Collection* of over 350 Victorian paintings in London, mislabeled as *The Foundry*. Christopher (Kip) Forbes, son of Malcolm Forbes (*Forbes Magazine* empire), built that collection as a thesis project starting in the 1960s and subsequently grew it into the most distinguished collection of Victorian paintings formed in the second half of the 20th century. It was housed in the Forbes family mansion *Old Battersea House*, overlooking the Thames, until 2003 when it was dissolved in London by Christie's auction house.

**Bierl, Willibald [German, *1913]: Ore Mining Around 1500 (after
Georg Agricola 1556), stained glass panel, 37.5×35 in., 1982, signed**

The content of this stained glass panel is reproduced from a woodcut published in a book on mining and processing of metal ore, by Georg Agricola in 1556. This early book was originally published in Latin and translated into English in 1910 by the future President of the United States, Herbert Hoover, and his wife. This glass panel depicts the washing of tin ore. To the left the ore is brought in pushcarts and dumped on the ground. The ore is washed in the water chute and the soiled water runs to a sump. The rocks and tin are placed in a sieve and washed again by repeatedly lowering the sieve into a water-filled barrel. Then the tin ore can be picked out from the various other materials.

Bierl, Willibald [German, *1913]: Medieval Smelter (after Georg Agricola 1556), stained glass panel, 37.5×35 in., 1982, signed

This stained glass panel is also taken from Agricola's book, published in 1556. Depicted here are two melting furnaces to process metal. The furnaces are charged from above with fuel, as well as the washed and fractured ore. The furnaces are fired from below. The left furnace shows a discharge of slag. In the foreground a worker transports larger pieces of ore in a wheelbarrow. At this time, the furnaces were already very complex structures with a fine-tuned system to regulate the humidity.

Bierl, Willibald [German, *1913]: Forge Around 1500 (after Georg Agricola 1556), stained glass panel, 37.5×35 in., 1982, signed

This stained glass panel is also derived from the previously described book by Agricola. Here the woodcut source depicts the technology of metal processing. With his face protected from the heat by a felt cloth, the master holds a vessel filled with iron ore, charcoal and lime, to be melted over the fire. To the right is a slag runoff. At the end of the process, a mass of iron remains in the vessel. These chunks of iron must be broken up with wooden hammers to separate the remaining slag and to compress them before they can be forged.

Bierl, Willibald [German, *1913]: Cannon Foundry (after J. F. Weir), stained glass panel, 37.5×43 in., 1982, signed

The content of this stained glass window is borrowed from the painting by the American artist John Ferguson Weir, now owned by the *Putnum Historical Society,* Cold Springs, N.Y. The painting itself is illustrated on page 20 of the introductory chapter. The mold for the cannon is embedded deep in the foundry sand floor. A large ladle containing the molten metal is positioned over the mold with the assistance of a crane winch, visible to the right of the ladle. The liquid iron is poured into the cannon mold. Because of the grave danger associated with any flaws, the casting of cannon barrels was a rare art. The techniques were held in strict secrecy. Yet, even in those days, espionage and treason for profit were common.

Bierl, Willibald [German, *1913]: Munich Bell Founder,
stained glass panel, 37.5×35 in., 1982, signed

Until fairly recently, cannon and bell castings were usually produced by the same specialty foundries. In his famous *Book of Trade Guilds*, published in 1698, Christoph Weigel shows a "parts and bell foundryman" with a cast-iron cannon barrel and a cast metal bell (see left page). Prior to this time, bells were cast by monks. The bell foundryworker in this stained glass window is removing the "coat," or outer clay layer, from a newly cast bell. At the top of the bell are six metal pieces called risers, the result produced by pouring molten metal into the solidifying bell. These risers will be cut off during the finishing process. The figure behind the new bell illustrates the preparation of molten metal in a crucible for the next casting. The worker brings the firewood, while in the far background are the two steeples of *Frauenkirche*, a Munich landmark. Dr. Grohmann commissioned this stained glass window in 1982 for this stained glass series of the most traditional foundry methods and products. It is an artist's idealistic impression of a bell-making operation, and not to be interpreted as an actual foundry operation.

Höchofen, Anfang 18. Jh.

Bierl, Willibald [German, *1913]: Blast Furnace (after Jan Brueghel), stained glass panel, 37.5×35 in., 1982, signed

In 1610, Jan Brueghel the Elder painted *Blast Furnace in the Forest*, the model for this stained glass panel. In the center, fire and tapped molten iron are flowing out of the blast furnace. A water reservoir to wash the ore is on the left. An overshot water wheel powers the bellows to supply air to the blast furnace. Behind the hut, stairs lead to the charging platform above the top of the blast furnaces, where ore, coal and lime are thrown into the furnaces. The ore is piled in the foreground.

1.2 Mining and Metals in the Industrial Age

Coal, Oil and Gas
Landscapes and Production Technologies

The largest subset of the ECKHART G. GROHMANN COLLECTION covers iron and steel production in the industrial age. For about 200 years, the mining, production and processing of metals have been the major driving forces of the economy. These activities have also had a strong influence on culture. Artists have interacted with these economic activities from their very beginning. The result is a wide spectrum of work portraying landscapes, technology, manufacturing processes and even work itself. The ambivalence of this historical period is illustrated by art that expresses admiration of these areas along with a great deal of skepticism.

Langer, Viggo [German, 1860-1953]: Oil Rigs in Baku at Caspian Sea, oil on canvas, 18×29 in., 1911, signed

The region around Baku in Azerbaijan is among the richest oil reserves in the world. Langer paints a landscape already crowded with drilling rigs at the beginning of the 20th century. Today this area is an exploited industrial landscape, largely devoid of its natural beauty. Even in this painting, children with no other choice play in the shadow of the oil wells. The painting can be seen as an early historical study of ecological issues.

Senger, Felix: Surface Soft Coal Mining With Electric Power Plant and Industry, oil on canvas, 35×55 in., 1939, signed

Soft coal is the product of ancient forests. Somewhat harder soft coal containing a higher carbon and reduced water content is usually mined in open pits. Germany has been, and continues to be, one of the major consumers of this coal. Its primary role is to power the turbines for the production of electricity. As illustrated by Senger, it is very advantageous to locate power plants in the vicinity of open coal pits. Here a narrow gage train transports the coal directly from the pit to the power plant. The Haag picture, to the right, features workers pushing soft coal in a cart on rails, with an electric power plant in the background. Mechanical drag lines were utilized in open pit mining

Keller, Erich [*1903]: Giant Dragline 240, Soft Coal Strip
Mining, Pit Jonny Scheer I, oil on canvas, 31.5×59 in.

Haag, Wilhelm [1907-1944]: Industrial Landscape with Two
Workers Pushing Lorry, oil on canvas, 33×55.5 in., signed

and were built increasingly larger as production capacity increased. Keller presents a large, complex machine of this kind. Technical advances of this type increased efficiency and replaced many workers, but allowed the burning of soft coal to remain competitive. However, in spite of many improvements, this operation is not without environmental implications. Soft coal deposits are spread over large areas and have required the transplanting of many villages to accommodate additional mining.

**Senghaas, Hermann: Gas Vessel and Industry, oil on
canvas, 17×21 in., monogrammed "H. S."**

Here we see an industrial landscape in winter, typically
found in the industrial area of the Ruhr Valley in Germany. The wintry industrial atmosphere of the town is
reflected in this composition of mining towers in the
background, interspersed with workshops and apartment
buildings, and a large gas storage tank at the optical center. These large round storage tanks maintained a constant
gas line pressure and were relatively common. They were
sealed internally with asphalt. Some of them remain today
as historical monuments. Others have been recycled and
renovated, employing the large round space to offer cultural events in an interesting setting.

Barth, Ferdinand [German, 1902-1979]: Boiler-house With Workers and Pumps, oil on canvas, 25×37 in., ca. 1935, signed

This painting is of a facility that provides hot water to an industrial plant. The picture shows surface condensers in which returning water under pressure is heated to 180 °F and then circulated by the pumps in the lower section of the painting to its proper use. Such installations were used in the paper and textile industries. [Thanks to *Caliqua AG*, Basel, Switzerland.]

Boscheiner (?): Upper-Silesia Coking Plant and Steel Mill, Germany, oil on canvas, 46.5×67 in., signed

A red-hot coke cake is pushed out of two coking chambers at the left. A workman quenches the material with a stream of water. The coke already quenched is deposited at the left foreground. Chamber gates are moved hydraulically. At top left is a blast furnace together with the associated machinery house. In front of them is the inclined skip hoist reaching the top of a blast furnace. The hemispherical domes of the recuperators are clear at the right of the canvas.

Dänike, Willi [German, 1903-1956]: Hosing Down the Coke, oil on canvas, 32.5×47 in., signed

The coke cake is just being pushed out. A workman begins the quenching process. An entire line of coking facilities extends across the left half of the painting. A line of coking ovens is shown along the right of the painting. These ovens have disgorged their coke, now cooled and awaiting transport to a blast furnace. A cloud of carbon dioxide gas is still hissing from the coke. In the left foreground, workers load the cooled coke onto railroad cars. In the background are three recuperators associated with a blast furnace. A bleeding of gases from a blast furnace is at the top right of the scene.

Gieshof, Josef: Hosing Down the Coke, oil on cardboard, 20.5×17 in., 1937, signed

Coke is created by heating coal in a low-oxygen environment in order to increase the heating value of the coal and thus reach higher temperatures in blast furnaces. Here the new coke is pushed out of two chambers of the battery of ovens. The hot coke catches fire when exposed to air and two men are busy quenching the degassed coke with water. Two additional workers break the coke cake into a pile. The plant's water reservoir tank is in the right background.

The Miners

Constantin-Emile Meunier is unquestionably the most important 19th century Belgian artist dealing with the subject of work. Both a painter and sculptor, he depicted the work and living conditions of Belgian miners and metalworkers as no one else had done. It was not until the late 1880s that his attention was drawn to this theme, while traveling to the heavy industrial district of Borinage. From then on he devoted his energy and creativity to portraying his impressions in paintings and sculptures.

Meunier was less interested in the technical documentation aspect of industrial work; he was much more interested in honoring the worker. Technical presentation is completely absent in his work. As Vincent van Gogh did at the same time, Meunier glorified the hard- working human being. He honored labor as the God-given fate of humans; no criticisms of society are generated. And yet, we find double meaning with Meunier. In his paintings he often emphasizes the heavy burden of extreme working conditions,

Meunier, Constantin-Emile [Belgian, 1831-1905]: The Miners, oil on canvas, 41×23.5 in., signed

while in his sculptures he glorifies the workers.

However, there is a third aspect to be considered with Meunier. While he shows workers during their free time, as in the painting on this page, they always exude a satisfied and relaxed mood. The workers are rooted in the culture of their living and working environment and this environment gives them their identity and self-esteem. In no way does Meunier portray a revolutionary proletariat as might be expected during this period of industrial conflict. The self-esteem emanating from this painting of the ECKHART G. GROHMANN COLLECTION is rooted in the regional culture and is sustained by the workers' knowledge of their importance to the industrial prosperity of the country.

In his later work, Meunier attempts a synthesis of all his art with the theme of work by creating a monument to work. Because of political shenanigans, he did not live to see its construction. It was only in the 1930s that this monument was finally erected in Brussels.

Meunier, Constantin-Emile [Belgian, 1831-1905]: Miners From the Borinage, Belgium, charcoal on paper, 21×17 in., entitled and signed "mineurs au borinage, C Meunier"

The examples on this double page are typical of the Belgian painter Meunier's images of miners. All the individuals are portrayed in a quiet and serious manner. One can see the hard labor in the faces of these miners. Although slim with protruding cheekbones, Meunier's miners are not desperate. They exude the characteristic dignity with which Meunier expressed his highest regard for their work. These miners are not the "heroes of work" found among some of Meunier's contemporaries and especially common in the generation that followed him.

Meunier, Constantin-Emile [Belgian, 1831-1905]:
Head of a Miner, bronze, 6.5×8.5 in., signed

Meunier, Constantin-Emile [Belgian, 1831-1905]: Head of a
Miner, bronze, 12.5×11 in., signed

Meunier, Constantin-Emile [Belgian, 1831-1905]: The Old Miner, bronze, 19 in., signed

An old miner, weary from a lifetime of hard physical labor underground, presents himself with his pickax and mining lamp. In spite of all his hardships, he has maintained an erect posture and exhibits his individuality with a certain self-confidence and pride. This presentation is typical of Meunier's expressive simplicity, in contrast to many of his contemporaries.

Beck, E. [German, 19th c.]: Miner, bronze, 18 in., signed

Levasseur, Henri Louis [French, *1853]: Miner, bronze, 16 in., signed

A miner with a pickax in his right hand carefully examines a piece of rock or coal.

This miner just finished a stroke with his pickax. The sculptor depicts an exhausted body, also indicated by the unusual bare feet.

**Küppers, Albert Hermann [German, *1842]: Miner,
bronze, 14 in., signed**

The three examples on these pages are figures of iron ore miners. The statues show the typical miner outfit, designed for their safety in leather with heavy-duty boots. The logo of their mining company is embossed on their clothing.

Additional equipment is a pickax and a lamp. The miner to the center examines a rock sample for its ore content. All three statues are idealized figures, meant to represent positive aspects of the miner. The actual difficult, dirty and

Reusch, Johann Friedrich [German, 1843-1906]: Iron Miner From the Siegerland, Germany, cast zinc, 25 in., signed

Küppers, Albert Hermann [German, *1842]: Miner, cast zinc, 25 in., signed

dangerous underground work depicted in Meunier's images is not apparent here. Many countries have created a widespread representation of art and culture raising the efforts of miners to a highly valued level. This can be seen as an attempt to compensate them for the hard reality of mining.

Kattop, Hans: Miner at Hard Work Underground, oil on canvas, 35×29 in., 1952, signed

Until World War I, underground coal was mined with a pickax and explosives. After 1918, machines began to replace what had been purely manual labor. Two of the most important new tools were the air hammer and the air drill, both powered by compressed air and seen in the paintings on these two pages. The miner to the left uses a small air hammer, one that he can handle easily by himself. The painting to the right shows a heavy drill unit requiring a

**Sieberg, Ottwill: Two Miners With Heavy Hammer
Drill, oil on canvas, 23.6×19.7 in.**

pair of miners to operate. Yet, in spite of technical innovation, work underground remained difficult and physically demanding. After World War II, comprehensive automatic mining machines increasingly carried the load. In many countries, manual labor gave way to machines.

Skála, Karel [Czech, *1908]: Three Miners in the Shaft,
oil on canvas, 45.5×57.5 in., signed

Here is a view into a mine tunnel supported by timber beams. Timber beams were preferred for underground support because, in the event of collapse, the timber would break and the cracking noise would warn the miners of imminent danger. Two miners shovel loosened coal into the track cart pushed by a third miner. The cart will move towards the mineshaft and then be lifted to the surface. The painter attempts to portray the underground atmosphere by simple artistic means such as color, shadows and inclination.

**G.U.S., monogrammed: Two Workers Filling Lorry
Underground, oil on canvas, 23.5×31.5 in.**

At an underground loading station, carts are loaded with freshly mined coal that was gathered in the tunnels, and is now reloaded down a chute. The miners still handle the carts manually and not by horse or engine power, as is common today.

**Küpper, Will [German, 1893-1972]: Advancing the
Tunnel, oil and pastel, 16×22 in., signed**

The miners are busily at work in an underground mine. Two men are extending the railroad tracks, while a third person is enlarging the opening. A skip can be detected at the left. The final section of a fresh air duct is discernible at the top of the painting. The construction site is illuminated by means of electric lighting, but the miners are also using their individual portable lamps.

**Gieshof, Josef: Beginning and Ending the Work Shift,
oil on cardboard, 20.5×17 in., 1937, signed**

An intermediate shaft connects two tunnel levels when the distance to the main shaft is too great. The pulley, wheels and wires transporting the elevator baskets can be seen. Beyond that, an underground ceiling encloses the area. It is shift change time. The workers of the completed shift leave the lower portion of the lift area. The entering shift workers crowd in front of the upper level, near the elevator basket. To the lower right you see a work cart used for the transport of the mined materials.

Dresse, Fernand [1916-1992]: After the Mine Accident, oil on canvas, 86.5×134 in., signed

Mines have been inherently dangerous from their very beginnings. Many miners lost their lives through accidents in the underground mines of the past, particularly gas explosions, water breaks and mine shaft collapses. The painter Fernand Dresse chose such a mine disaster as his subject for this highly unusual painting. Normally the focus of an underground disaster is on the recovery of the dead miners and the bereavement of the families. Dresse depicts the scene of digging and preparation of graves in a cemetery, in the midst of the mining landscape. Digging continues at one end of the grave while a miner is lowered to his rest at the other end. With this painting Dresse created a most impressive scene of quiet work as the last service to the fallen miners.

Kalish, Max [American, 1891-1945]: The Stoker, bronze, 21 in., signed, foundrymark "Meroni-Radice cire perdue Paris"

Anonymous: Stoker, bronze, 9.5 in., inscribed "Verband der Gemeinde und Staatsarbeiter gegründet 1896"

The stoker represented a very popular subject for American sculptors. His activities symbolized extreme physical labor. Such figures of workers are typical of Max Kalish. His workers are usually men of action. This stoker, however, is at rest and presented in a victor's pose. He could be a worker servicing a boiler, such as the stoker shown in the drawing at right by Swedish artist Stoopendahl. The bronze stoker above on the right, by an anonymous artist, holds a coal shovel in addition to the required steel rod.

Furnaces and Smelters
Views of Steel Mills

Mercker, Erich [German, 1891-1973]: Coal Mine and
Coking Plants, oil on canvas, 23×31 in., 1966, signed

The center of this painting is characterized by the glaring red glow of the degassed hard coal that is just being expelled. Just to the right, yellow flaring gases are discernible from the coking chambers still in operation. A train with several wagons and a steam engine stands ready to carry the quenched coke. To the left of the coking chambers, beyond the approaching steam engine, there are gas pipe-lines containing gas generated by the coking operation. At the right side of the painting are the elevator systems at the head of the coal mine. The charging machines for the coke ovens are also at the right. Two chimneys in the background belong to a power plant providing the electrical energy needed to operate the mine.

Mercker, Erich [German, 1891-1973]: Bird's-Eye View of Large Steel Mills at Schalke, Germany, oil on canvas, 38.5×46.5 in., signed

At the left of this painting is a line of blast furnaces. A tapping operation is taking place at the plant in the very forefront. An open hearth furnace is visible at the right center of the painting. Liquid steel is being run off there as well. The frame at the head of a coal mine pit can be identified in the foreground at the center of the painting. A raised railroad track runs across the river at the top left of the canvas.

Mercker, Erich [German, 1891-1973]: Blast Furnaces
on Ruhr River, Germany, oil on canvas, 24×34 in., 1962,
signed

A blast furnace is being tapped off at the center right. In the middle of the painting is the casting heap together with the pig iron bed to receive the output of the blast furnace. To the right are three trolley cars to convey the cooled down pig iron. A lift tower for charging the left blast furnace rises above the locomotive. A service crane operates at the top of the furnace. A small control room for the operation of the intramill railway is seen just above cargo cars on the mill tracks. The high chimneys in the background serve the operation of the Siemens-Martin plant.

Mercker, Erich [German, 1891-1973]: Evening
Atmosphere at Blast Furnaces in Mülheim/Ruhr,
Germany, oil on canvas, 23×31 in., 1963, signed

The tapping of a blast furnace can be seen at the center rear of this painting. Another tapping has just been completed at the left foreground. Apparently the edges of the pig iron bed have already cooled down. In the foreground is a plant railway carrying slag ladles to the blast furnace. Two vents are visible at the top of the blast furnace for burning off excess top gas. To the left are two recupera-tors. In these recuperators, the blast furnace top gases are employed to heat up the fresh air, which is then conveyed to the blast furnace base to aid the combustion process. At center right of the painting is the outline of a winch house for operating the inclined skip hoists to supply the charge to the blast furnaces. The slender, tall chimneys belong to the gas-fired Siemens-Martin furnaces.

Mercker, Erich [German, 1891-1973]: Evening at the Blast Furnace, oil on canvas, scraper tech., 25×33 in., ca. 1920-30, signed

A foundry bay including newly cast pig iron just being quenched is in the foreground. Two recuperators are to the right. A steam engine is approaching the center of the plant. At the top of the blast furnace at the center, the tilting mechanism of the top gas bell clearly stands out against the smoke-covered sky. Beside the blast furnace is a hoist for lifting the charging materials. An auxiliary crane operates at the top of the blast furnace at the upper left of the painting.

Mercker, Erich [German, 1891-1973]: Large Steel Mill, oil on canvas, 31×43 in., signed

This painting depicts a steel plant including several blast furnaces. A line of blast furnaces is clear at the left center of the painting. The second blast furnace on the left side and the furnace on the right side are being charged with raw materials. This is indicated by the release of top gases painted in a dark color. The last of the furnaces in the background is being bled, as indicated by the flame.

A steam locomotive pulling a train is approaching on the central railroad track. The hemispherical domes of the recuperators can be discerned near the blast furnaces. In the foundry hall at the base of the first blast furnace, the pig iron is still glowing after a recent tapping operation. In front are several railroad cars.

Mercker, Erich [German, 1891-1973]: Industrial Ruhr District, Germany, oil on canvas, 23.5×31.5 in., 1966, signed

This painting depicts a large steel mill in the German industrial district on the Ruhr River. Two blast furnaces occupy the left of the picture. The inclined charging elevators used to lift the raw materials are clearly visible. Recuperators stand in the front of each blast furnace, ready to preheat the needed fresh air. Chimneys tower over the steel processing buildings at the right of the painting. For many years chimneys were the symbols of economic prosperity. The tracks of the rail system providing transportation within the steel mill complex can be seen at the right.

Mercker, Erich [German, 1891-1973]: Places of Work:
Iron- and Steelworks, oil on cardboard, 16×19 in.,
signed

This Mercker painting provides an excellent impression of the dirty operation of a blast furnace. In the right bottom corner, a company steam engine is moving three raw material carts. Above them, the right section of the painting depicts the structure of a blast furnace. Closer to the center, several workers service two cargo carts carrying building materials. Through the clouds of smoke the viewer can identify the silhouette of another blast furnace. In the left foreground is a foundry bay with pig iron ingots that have cooled. At the far left, contours of recuperators become visible. The fiery glow from a runoff operation at a neighboring blast furnace can be discerned beyond the front tapping platform.

Mercker, Erich [German, 1891-1973]: Tapping a Blast
Furnace at Mülheim/Ruhr, Germany, oil on canvas,
23×31 in., signed

The tapping of a blast furnace (background) can be identified by the glowing pig iron at the lower center of this painting. In front of the blast furnace, there is heavy works traffic commotion being carried out by means of several steam engines. To the left of the blast furnace is a pig iron bed already fairly well cooled. To the left of the blast furnace are huge pipelines to supply top gas and fresh air into the blast furnaces. At the left of the painting are the recuperators for preheating the air supply for the two blast furnaces. At the top of the blast furnace is the tilting chute used to open and close the top gas bells. A forest of chimneys to the right of the painting belongs to a Siemens-Martin plant.

Mercker, Erich [German, 1891-1973]: Blast Furnace, oil on canvas, 45.5×39.5 in., 1963, signed

This blast furnace is undergoing extensive maintenance and repair. New sections of pipe have been delivered and await installation. The blast furnace is shut down during the repair operation. The second blast furnace in the line is being tapped. The in-plant railroad engine can avoid the construction site by utilizing the track switches. A rail car loaded with a slag pot stands ready to be picked up. The tapped metal is discharged onto the pig iron cooling floor, covered by sand.

Mercker, Erich [German, 1891-1973]: Steel Mill,
Dortmund, Germany, oil on canvas, 23.5×31.5 in., 1957,
signed

The blast furnaces standing next to one another in this painting have a common casting bay. A tapping operation is taking place at one blast furnace. The pig iron is poured into a sand bed. The blast furnaces have inclined skip hoists. In the right section of the painting, flue gas is bled at the top of a tower. Next to the tower is a lower water tower containing nonpotable water for industrial use. Both the chimneys on the right are part of an open-hearth steel plant. The steam-powered company railroad operates below the water tower. In front of the buildings in the left foreground is a water basin filter for the purification of the process water.

Mercker, Erich [German, 1891-1973]: Blast Furnace at Duisburg-Hamborn, Germany, oil on canvas, 23.5×31.5 in., 1963, signed

The tapping operation has been completed. A company steam engine is pulling a train of five slag cars. The hot liquid slag glows at the center of the painting. At the right of the canvas are three recuperators. Another set of recuperators can be identified in the center background. The blast furnace on the left is linked with the recupera-tors via huge flue ducts. Three furnace workers are shown operating in the vicinity of the top gas platform. The blast furnace is of an older design that features a rail mounted tilting device. Two pipelines for the bleeding of excess blast furnace gas extend to the top edge of the painting.

**Mercker, Erich [German, 1891-1973]: Blast Furnaces
on Ruhr River, Germany, oil on canvas, 23.5×31.5 in.,
1967, signed**

In this painting a railroad Y-track runs in front of a line of blast furnaces. The traffic of moving material around the plant is hectic. Two steam engines pulling cargo cars are shown at work. A blast furnace has just been tapped. The glow of hardening pig iron illuminates the center of the scene. At the center of the painting a cooling tower releases steam. Three recuperators appear to be attached to its right side. Towards the river, the piping of additional blast furnaces becomes visible. Two derrick cranes are at the river bank. Yet another iron and steel plant is operating on the opposite bank of the Rhein River. Inside this distant steel mill, a tapping operation is also underway. Two more recuperators are visible along the left edge of the painting. At the top of both center blast furnaces, the excess gas burners are in use, bleeding off the flue gas. At the front blast furnace, the rocking device controlling the flue-gas bell lifting soars into the dirty skies.

Mercker, Erich [German, 1891-1973]: Friedrich-
Wilhelm-Hütte, Steel Mill, Mülheim, Germany, oil on
academy board, 16×20 in., signed

The sand bed for generating pig iron ingots is being quenched outside a line of four blast furnaces. In front of these blast furnaces is a mill railway operated by a steam engine, ready to convey the pig iron production. To the very left of the painting is the hemispherical hood of a recuperator. Next to the recuperator is the rope guide with two large guide rolls for the transportation of the burdening. The blast furnaces are connected by large-scale pipelines to supply the blast furnace gas and the fresh air for the melting process. The vents for burning off excess top gas can be seen at the top of each blast furnace. At the immediate right of the last blast furnace, a flaring operation is underway. The production of steam above the building to the lower right center indicates the operation of a coking plant. The chimney discernible to its left is part of the coking plant as well. The water canal to the right in the painting is used to transport the required steel work materials by ship: ore, coal and lime. The unloading is arranged via two clearly visible cranes.

Mercker, Erich [German, 1891-1973]: Blast Furnaces
#2 and #3, Herrenwyk, Germany, oil on academy board,
15.5×19.5 in., ca. 1955, signed

In the foreground, a crane is displayed along with railroad wagons carrying building materials. A blast furnace under construction is at the center, while an operational blast furnace is to the right. Top gases flare at the top platform.

The major pipeline to the left at the center of the picture supplies combustion air to the base of the blast furnace. The conveying of charging materials via inclined skip hoists for both blast furnaces is clearly visible.

Ehrenberg, Paul [German, 1876-1949]: Neunkirchen
Steel Mill, Saarland, Germany, oil on canvas, 30×35 in.,
ca. 1930, signed

The plant gate with a distinctive gatehouse on a mill street occupies the foreground of this painting. A rubber-lined cargo wagon drawn by two horses moves along the street. A few workmen are seen at several locations at the gate and along the street. Two blast furnaces are at the center of the painting. One can identify three recuperators to the right. The fiery glow of the liquid pig iron released by the blast furnace is reflected in the roof of the foundry building.

Jantzen, F. [German]: Westphalian Steel Mill With Railway, Germany, oil on canvas, 23×31 in.

The two blast furnaces at the left of this painting are of different size and age. The older, smaller furnace has just been tapped. The reflected glow of the molten pig iron deposited on the sand floor is very visible. The blast furnace is equipped with a vertical elevator to supply the charge to the top of the furnace. The newer, larger blast furnace to the far left features the more modern inclined elevator. Both furnaces include vent pipes to burn off excess gas. A parallelogram linkage superstructure, designed to open the coal gas bell at the top of the furnace, encloses the smaller furnace. The steam-powered railway engine provides in-plant transportation. Three recuperators stand to the right center background, ready to preheat the blast furnace air.

Mercker, Erich [German, 1891-1973]: The Erection of a
Blast Furnace in Linz (Austria), oil on chipboard, 15×19
in., signed

The flue gas main leading from the top gas collector has already been assembled. Behind the blast furnace frame is the inclined skip hoist. To the right stands a single recuperator with a distinctive hemispherical bell. Between the skip hoist and the recuperator is the winchgear house. In the foreground a company steam engine is moving four railroad cars carrying construction materials. The delivery of construction materials is accomplished via the railroad tracks. Several pipe sections lie in the foreground ready to be assembled. At the left of the painting, a water tower is about to be completed. The blue spots in the painting relate to workmen wearing their boiler suits. Another field railroad is operating at the left of the painting.

Schlichting, Max [German, 1866-1937]: At the Ruhr River, Evening Atmosphere at Furnaces With Rails, oil on canvas, 40×60 in., ca. 1910, signed

A Siemens-Martin steel plant is located at the right of this painting. At the center is the casting house where the newly produced steel is cast into blocks. The casting room is filled with the fiery glow of the molten steel.

The black yard engine pulls a used steel mold out of the casting house. A well-lit switching station stands in the foreground. The two hemispherically-topped recuperator towers are associated with the blast furnace.

Dongen, G.: **Blast Furnace With Locomotive,** oil on canvas, 33×25 in., signed.

At the center of this painting stands a blast furnace with a set of preheating recuperators. The circular pipe with a strikingly large cross section serves as an inlet of preheated fresh air to the base of the furnace. The blast furnace is just being bled. The flaring flames are clearly discernible at the top edge of the painting. Two bleeding facilities belong to the blast furnace nearby, which is currently not operating. This picture is a copy of a painting by Heinrich Kley.

**Paetzold: Steel Mill Row, oil on cardboard, 20×14 in.,
signed**

This painting is dominated by a blast furnace at the right center and a row of air preheaters at the left center. A railroad track runs between the two installations to provide the raw materials such as iron ore, coal, coke and lime to the blast furnace. A railroad shed is in the background. The blast furnace is encased in an elaborate superstructure, particularly at the top. The superstructure's purpose is probably related to the charging process of the blast furnace.

H.B.: Blast Furnace, oil on canvas, 23×18 in., ca.
1940-50, monogrammed

This painting shows a blast furnace facility in substantial detail. The blast furnace in the center is enclosed in a framework that extends to another furnace immediately behind the first. The structure extends above the blast furnaces and enables the control of charging and venting process. A group of four recuperators stands at the left and the furnaces are both tapped in the building at the right. A group of workers in the foreground repair a track problem on the in-plant railroad.

Müller, Hans: Duisburg Copper Mill, Oil on canvas
32×40 in., ca. 1920-40, signed

The processing of copper is similar in many ways to the production of pig iron. However, the pollution caused by exhausted impurities can be much worse. Charging of the blast furnace on the right is done by the sloping lift while a vertical elevator charges the left blast furnace. Between the two blast furnaces are the recuperators. The left blast furnace is being tapped to release the glowing molten copper. Both furnaces show an exhaust gas vent and are equipped to burn off gases.

Anonymous: Arc Furnace, oil on canvas, 27×20 in.

The electric arc furnace conveys an almost menacing impression due to the distortion of perspective. The furnace has been tilted backwards for a pouring operation. The three electrodes have been raised. The electrodes still glow and project from the electrode bridge above. Together with the open charging orifice, the scene evokes the image of a monster. The implements lying around in the foreground are reduced to a state of insignificance.

Skell, Fritz [German, 1885-1961]: Foundry With Workers, oil on canvas, 40.5×50.5 in., 1935, signed

Fritz Skell depicts an electric arc furnace with its attending workers in this painting. An electric arc formed between electrode and metal (scrap) creates the heat that produces the molten steel. The three electrodes of the arc furnace are withdrawn, but visible in the background.

The furnace is tipped forward and the molten steel pours into the transfer ladle. The steelworkers carry the large steel bars used to remove the slag. They must endure tremendous heat.

Gaspari: Pouring Off Slag, oil on canvas, 15.5×21 in., ca. 1961, signed

The railroad track has been laid along the top of the slag heap and can be extended further as the growing heap requires. This painting shows two slag cars. At the right side of the canvas, the slag has already been poured off. The slag ladle is tilted by means of a threaded spindle. This operation is depicted at the second car. In modern steelmaking, liquid slag is mostly used for making paving stones and other byproducts. Slag containing phosphorus is turned into Thomas meal. A complex of blast furnaces can be seen in the background of the painting.

Interiors: Technology and Workers

Montan, Anders [Swedish, 1846-1917]: At the Blast Furnace, oil on cardboard, 10×8 in., signed

The blast furnace tapping is underway. Newly discharged pig iron floats along the runner at the right of the painting. Only the apparel of the blast furnace worker at the center meets professional and safety requirements. The pulley above the three workers controls the plug to stop the flow. Activating the pulley causes a lump of refractory material to be forced into the orifice of the blast furnace to seal it until later in the process.

Neuerburg, Gerhard [German, 1872-1946]: Steel Mill With Bessemer Pear, oil on canvas, 17×23 in., signed

The center of this painting shows a Bessemer converter during the blowing operation, where air is forced into the bottom of the pear-shaped vessel. By means of two large geared wheels the converter can be turned after the blowing process. To the left in the painting are two cupola furnaces in operation. From the right furnace the already molten iron is discharging and entering into the transfer ladle, suspended from the hook of a crane. In the foreground of this foundry bay, two hemispherical molds are being prepared for casting.

Zirgel, W. [German, †1930]: At the Furnace, oil on canvas, 30×37 in.

The Siemens-Martin open-hearth furnace has been charged with scrap metal. The steelworkers at the center of the painting are busy distributing the load evenly inside the furnace using their long stokers. The function of the large slab in front of the charged opening is probably a heat shield for the crew. At the upper center, a hot metal charge ladle hangs from a crane. At the right edge of the picture are two charge buckets.

Dehn, G.: Tapping the Furnace, oil on cardboard, 18×25.5 in., ca. 1900, signed

In this painting three workers tap a blast furnace to remove the liquid metal. They stand next to a trough lined with firebrick and remove slag pieces with their iron rods as they flow by. A ramming device to close the tap with a plug is hanging on a track running overhead. Safety clothing protects the workers from the intense heat and hot iron sparks.

Korthaus, Carl A. [1879-1956]: Tapping Off Slag, oil on cardboard, 16.5×23 in., signed

This picture shows the tapping platform, the location where the liquid iron is released from the blast furnace. The painter has taken a great deal of artistic license. A steelworker to the right has a tool in the flowing stream of molten pig iron. A cleaning lady tries to contain the foam layer that covers the platform. A blower pipe to supply air to the blast furnace snakes around like a python at the upper edge of the painting.

Mercker, Erich [German, 1891-1973]: Cable Plant,
Nuremberg, Germany, oil on academy board, 15×19 in.,
signed

The foreground of the bay is covered with annealing furnaces, where the drawn wire is heated to remove brittleness. At the center of the painting is the cable jacket press facility. Several coils of jacketed cable are placed around the press. Along the right edge of the painting a vertical short-stroke jolting machine can be seen which is designed to press blooms into bar-sized materials. Two overhead traveling cranes operate inside the workshop.

Scherban, Alexander [Austrian, 1886-1964]: **Open Hearth Steel Mill, Donawitz, Austria, watercolor on paper, 20×24.5 in., 1937, signed**

Alexander Scherban painted a substantial series of industrial scenes. Here he depicts the furnace charging platform of a steel mill. The charge board, which carries materials to be placed in the furnace, rides on wide steel tracks at the left background. The charge material arrives with the help of a turntable and enters the furnace through a rear door, shown in the right foreground. Three steelworkers distribute the charged material evenly within the furnace, using long iron bars.

Lepanova, L.: Tapping Slag at Blast Furnace, oil on canvas, 47×40 in., 1958, signed

This painting shows the release of liquid metal at the tapping platform of a blast furnace. Slag, consisting of impurities, runs into a slag pan placed on the transport cart in the left foreground, below the runoff lip. The background illustrates a pig iron pan being filled with the molten pig iron. Additional catwalks allowing access to the blast furnace are seen above this level. The two workers on the tapping platform are outfitted with protective asbestos suits.

Tylle, Hans Dieter [German, *1954]: Steel Mill, oil on canvas, 71×55 in., 1989, signed

Contemporary German artist Hans Dieter Tylle presents the interior of the Salzgitter AG steel mill in Germany. In the background, a bridge crane holds a tipping platform to charge a forced air steel pear furnace (Bessemer pear). To the right foreground is a slag pan. In the left foreground lies a furnace cover used for steel refinement by vacuum degassing. This painting provides a special appeal with its unusual composition of perspective and the interplay of fire and smoke in the background.

**Mercker, Erich [German, 1891-1973]: Ingot Casting,
oil on canvas, 30×36 in., signed**

Two casting pits in left foreground contain molds ready for the casting operation. At the center of the painting, a crane hoist supports a pouring ladle containing the molten steel. The casting process is underway and the liquid steel pours into the molds. The molds are linked to each other via ceramic tubes in the mold bed. A railroad track for the transportation of ingots can be seen at the side of the cast-ing shop. The ingots from the previous casting operation already are removed from their molds and loaded onto the railroad cars. Beyond the ingot cars inside the second nave of the hall, a stripping crane is holding an ingot in its tongs that has just been removed from a mold.

Korthaus, Carl A. [1879-1956]: Construction of Foundation for Blast Furnace, oil on cardboard, 17×21 in., signed

Transport carts for construction materials are shown in the foreground. The orange-red firebrick foundations appear very light in color, dependent on the specific clay content of the firebrick. The oval shape of the brick structure suggests a use, perhaps to inject the air into the blast furnace.

Anonymous: In the Iron Foundry, oil on canvas, 38×59 in., ca. 1920

A four-man crew pours molten steel into four ingot molds at floor level. The four molds are piped together at their bottoms in the pit. As one mold is filled, the molten steel rises equally in all four connected molds. With a long, hinged push rod, the caster to the left of the platform directs the metal stream to the middle of a floor mold. The middle of the floor mold is free of built-up metal spills and slag deposits.

Schmidt, H. [German]: Tapping Large Transfer Ladle (after Heinrich Kley), oil on canvas, 10×14 in., 1923, signed

Workers tap the right converter ladle. The stream of molten metal runs into an intermediate distribution ladle. The castinghouse worker at the center of the painting removes pieces of slag with a long steel rod. Then the molten steel runs down a trough leading to the ingot molds and other molds, as needed. Both ladles have easily identifiable stopper rods. The large spoked wheels control the tipping of the ladle for slag removal after the molten steel has been poured. The caster behind the slag remover directs the metal stream with his rod. To the left, at the edge of the picture, is worker with a sampling ladle. The safety glasses of the casters at the left center reflect away most of the bright light from the flowing molten steel.

Köhler, Fritz [German, 1850-1917]: Molten Metal Transfer Ladle, Ready to Pour Off, oil on canvas, 23×21 in., signed

The overhead bridge crane moves the transfer ladle to approximately the correct location. Three groups of steelworkers manually try to achieve a more precise position. The plug linkage at the top right rim of the transfer ladle indicates that the discharge plug is already open. The molten metal flows out of the ladle with a glaring white heat, and into molds positioned to receive the steel. Workers must employ the tilting device at the center of the ladle when lowering the ladle. Employing the tilting device simultaneously ensures that the slag remains inside the ladle, and the steel discharges properly.

**Authenstetter (?), Georg [German]: Brass Cast House,
oil on canvas, 39×51 in., 1937, signed**

A ladle for melting recycled brass parts is shown at the upper right of the painting. The energy for melting is provided by an electric arc furnace. An instrument panel for controlling the process is seen behind the ladle. At the center of the painting, brass streams from a ladle into a round mold to produce brass bars. These brass bars will continue to be worked in an extrusion press to become rods. The dies needed for this next process are lying to the left. A cast brass plate, not yet completely cooled, is suspended from an overhead crane by a pulley system. The scale of the exhaust facilities for handling the zinc fumes generated by the casting process is quite remarkable. The brass bar at the bottom right edge of the painting has been expelled from the mold. A second brass bar, still glowing, is about to be expelled.

**Losito, Luigi [Italian, 1905-1992]: Two Workers at
Blast Furnace, oil on panel, 36.5×26 in., 1951, signed**

Two workers stand in heroic poses in front of a preheating oven preparing steel to be rolled. The worker to the right holds tongs typically used in the rolling mill, while the other holds a hammer on his shoulder. In the left background, a group of workers wrestle a workpiece out of the furnace and toward the rolling mill to the right of the picture.

Janensch, Gerhard Adolf [German, 1860-1933]: Tall Puddler, bronze, 32 in., signed

This puddler holds a long iron rod with familiarity. He wears a hard hat for head cover, leather gloves, leather apron, and probably a shirt made of a leatherlike material. His shoes are outfitted with heavy soles. Puddling was a physically demanding task performed as a part of the steel production process (pages 36, 37). In close proximity to the hot melt furnace, the molten iron charge had to be stirred by steelworkers.

Meunier, Constantin-Emile [Belgian, 1831-1905]:
Resting Puddler, bronze, 15.5×9.5 in., 1890, signed

Constantin Meunier, in particular, created a memorial to the profession of the puddler worker. His famous sculpture of the resting puddler, later produced in various sizes, is an impressive monument depicting the extraordinarily heavy burden of this work activity.

FOUNDRIES, FORGE SHOPS AND ROLLING MILLS

Foundries: Ferrous and Nonferrous

A substantial portion of the ECKHART G. GROHMANN COLLECTION deals with the further processing of metals refined from ore. Casting, forging and rolling are the basic processes to bring the raw material close to the desired form and prepare it for additional processing. The handling of hot metal presents an attractive subject for artists.

Glowing iron, large machinery and heavy physical labor in an environment of heat, smoke and noise are the basic components of a dynamic ensemble of industrial production. While iron and steel are fairly common, it is rather rare to find the processing of nonferrous metals as an artistic subject. However, the following pages include some nonferrous examples.

Fuhry, Richard [German, 1882-1935?]: Foundry Interior, oil on cardboard, 27×38.5 in., 1914, signed

A casting operation is taking place at the center of the painting. Just in front, two workmen struggle to move a hexagonal bar mold. At the left edge, a crucible furnace; molten metal is discharged from it for the casting at the center of the canvas. The right section of the painting includes another crucible furnace. The melt is also extracted there. The smelter is taking a small ladle to fill up a long extended mold. In front of the runner there are a number of cast ingots.

**Schlicht, Carl von [German, 1833- after 1912]:
Graefenbach-Hütte, Iron Foundry, Böcking, Germany,
oil on canvas, 37.5×49 in., 1897, signed**

The Böcking Foundry manufactured iron castings. Scrap metal served as raw material and was purchased in the surrounding area. The iron to be recycled was taken to the mill on heavy, open carts drawn by the four draft horses. Additional raw material was purchased from blast furnace operators. This painting shows stacks of wood lying in the grass in front of the forest opening. A great deal of scrap metal is deposited outside the casting bay. The smelting furnace is located inside the taller building behind the casting shop. At the side of the casting bay there is a derrick with block and pulley for hauling heavy items.

Korthaus, Carl A. [1879-1956]: In the Foundry, oil on cardboard, 13×19 in., signed

Here is a view of the tapping of a cupola furnace in a foundry. This painting shows the trough guiding the molten metal into the transfer ladle. The trough's supporting steel superstructure hangs from the hook of the crane. At the side of the ladle is a handle used to control the tipping of the ladle when pouring molten metal into a sand mold. The cupola oven is charged from above.

Mercker, Erich [German, 1891-1973]: In the Foundry, oil on canvas, 23.5×31.5 in., 1969, signed

An empty transfer ladle hangs in the foreground, waiting to discharge its remaining slag. To its side and a little farther back, a slag ladle awaits. At the left of center, a casting ladle has poured its steel and is now tilted to allow the remaining slag to discharge into the slag ladle. Just to the left, a ladle has cooled down and been positioned horizontally to allow an examination of the brick lining. A large ladle, ready for casting, is found at the center of the painting. Several square molds are located in the foreground. Some empty mold frames or flasks also lie nearby. The background is brightly lit by the furnace house. Several cast products are visible in the neighboring bay.

Mercker, Erich [German, 1891-1973]: **Molding Before Casting, Gutehoffnungshütte, Germany**, oil on academy board, 16×18 in., signed

The yellow materials in the foreground of this painting may be fresh molding sand. To the right center stands a casting in the shape of a bridge. Four foundryworkers are busy in the middle of the picture. Two of them are concerned with the removal of residual slag from a foundry ladle. To their right, small and weak yellow flames indicate that a casting has just been completed. The crane at the right edge has a freshly filled casting ladle in its lifting tackle. At the left edge, a casting ladle filled with liquid steel tilts forward to pour.

Picco-Rückert, Ria [German, 1900-1967]:
Floormolding, oil on canvas, 23.2×17.3 in., 1942

The industrial painter Picco-Rückert illustrates the pouring of molten steel into large ingot molds. The ingot molds are mounted onto a common base plate, which rests on a heavy-duty rail car. The base plate has connecting pipes so that filling one mold automatically fills the others.

Haberecht, Georg [German]: Ingot Molds, Meissen
porcelain plaque, 12×10 in., ca. 1910, monogrammed "GH"

A casting ladle containing liquid steel is suspended above a series of molds. Molten steel pours into one of the molds. Since the molds inside the metal runner are linked to each other, the liquid level rises simultaneously in all the molds as the molten steel is poured. The casting supervisor positions the casting ladle, and thereby the casting stream, to prevent any possible spillage of the liquid steel. The workman at the left foreground is signaling a change in direction to the crane operator.

Wilke, Heinrich [German, *1869]: van Tongel's Steel
Works in Güstrow, Germany, oil on canvas, 39×59 in.,
1917, signed

The foundry in this painting is equipped with two cupola furnaces located to the left of the picture. From the top of a ladder, a workman supervises the combustion operation through a sight hole in the side of the furnace. Two bridge cranes travel above the foundry bay, capable of supporting casting ladles by a suspension tackle. A hook with an annular eye nests at the crossbeam of the casting ladle. A foundryworker has placed a steel bar through the eye which guides him to open the stopper of the cupola furnace. The liquid iron is discharging into the ladle. At the rear wall, a basic oxygen converter operates with a second converter along the same wall standing idle. The rightmost casting ladle involves three foundryworkers in the casting process. The middle laborer is opening the stopper rod mechanism. The other two workmen are positioning the casting jet leaving the ladle. The mill manager is supervising the casting operation. The gentleman to the right of the ladle, wearing a peaked cap, is the owner of the steelmill. His appearance is a common practice in industrial paintings.

Hinze, Walter [German, *1875]: Karl Krause Foundry
II, oil on panel, 14×31 in., 1955, signed

Hinze, Walter [German, *1875]: Karl Krause Foundry I,
oil on panel, 25×56 in., 1913, signed

Walter Hinze executed this painting in two versions. He painted the larger version first, and later created the smaller one for the company's anniversary. In a tradition common to industrial art, he placed the company owner and founder in the center of the later version. The painting itself shows a tapping of the cupola furnace. Two bridge cranes deliver the transfer ladles to fill the particularly large mold. The worker at the right foreground supervises the activity.

**Mercker, Erich [German, 1891-1973]: Interior of a
Sand Foundry, oil on cardboard, 14×18 in., signed**

Inside this foundry are a number of rectangular mold-ing boxes for sand casting. A conveyor belt runs across the foreground. Once the cast items have been released from their molds, the spent sand is put onto the conveyor belt and carried to the chute at the center foreground. Here the sand is loaded via the chute and taken to a sand regeneration plant. The bridge crane along the right edge of the picture spans across the entire casting bay. The mid-dle of the painting shows the tapping operation preceding the next casting process.

Staeger, Ferdinand [German, *1880]: Foundry Interior, watercolor, 12.5×18 in., signed

This foundry produces castings according to weight. The master founder has calculated the net weight by deducting the tare weight from the gross weight. Two runner gates project above the floor from the foundry pit, behind the scales. The crucible pan at the right edge of the picture already has been emptied. The casting ladle suspended from the crane by chains is also empty. The exhaust facility beyond the casting ladle has been moved aside for the casting operation. At the left background, a crucible pan can be seen. Several solidified flow gates lie on the floor in the foreground, waiting to be recycled.

Förster, Karol [Polish, *1902]: Aluminum Foundry, oil on canvas, 36×29 in., 1942, signed

This picture is a rare painting of an experimental aluminum foundry. At the left foreground, two workers pour molten aluminum into a closed mold held together in a steel flask, or frame. They use a large ladle supported by a forked, long-handled bar. Aluminum is one-third the weight of iron or steel, so a larger quantity of molten metal can be handled manually. In the background, a red-hot crucible filled with molten aluminum is pulled out of a crucible furnace with the assistance of a crane. The worker in the middle skims the surface of a melt bath and places the dross, consisting of oxides and impurities, into a dross bucket. The lower right center shows a finished open mold half in a steel flask containing the half shape of a new part. The two finished halves are called the "cope" (upper) and "drag" (lower) parts of an assembled mold. In the right lower corner is a pile of loose, green sand, with a shovel and a round sieve. These are used to distribute the green sand evenly inside the steel flask around the pattern. Above is an empty melting crucible. All the foundryworkers show the intense concentration needed for their work.

Tylle, Hans Dieter [German, *1954]: Electrolysis Bay, Aluminum Works Isal, Island (Study), oil on cardboard, 12×15.5 in., 1991, signed

These two oil studies were sketched by H.D. Tylle inside an aluminum reduction plant in Iceland. They illustrate a row of reduction pots (electric melting furnaces) in which pure aluminum metal is produced by the electrolysis of a solution of alumina in molten fluorides. Aluminum is the most abundant metallic element in the earth's crust, having a nearly 8-percent share. Processing reduces bauxite ore to alumina, a crystalline substance of pure aluminum oxide, resembling refined sugar. This alumina oxide is transported to the charging wells of these electrolytic reduction cells. The reduction process separates the aluminum metal from the oxygen. This continuous process is very energy intensive and produces one pound of pure aluminum from two pounds of alumina. The molten aluminum is periodically siphoned off to transfer ladles carried by the carts shown. The transfer ladles pour the aluminum into ingot molds as it is being transferred to the next stage of processing. [E.G. Grohmann]

Tylle, Hans Dieter [German, *1954]: Electrolysis Bay, Aluminum Works Isal, Island (Study), oil on cardboard, 10×12 in., 1991, signed

Paintings of the *Aluminum Casting & Engineering Co.* (ACE/CO), Milwaukee, Wisconsin by H.D. Tylle
Descriptions by Dr. E.G. Grohmann, Chairman and President

The industrial painter, H.D. Tylle (Kassel, Germany) visited the *Aluminum Casting & Engineering Company* (ACE/CO) in Milwaukee, Wis., in May 2002. The ACE/CO foundry produces aluminum castings for the automotive industry. At various locations in the plant, Tylle painted seven oil studies using prepared, white cardboard on a tripod easel. He quickly sketched the oil studies, each within a few hours. These oil sketches serve to capture the industrial atmosphere. The scenes were simultaneously photographed to capture additional details for later reference as Tylle prepares the final, larger paintings in his studio in Kassel, Germany.

Tylle, Hans Dieter [German, *1954]: Core Production, ACE/CO, Milwaukee, oil on canvas, 35.5×47 in., 2003, signed

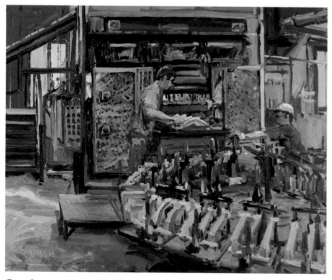

Study to *Core Production*, ACE/CO, Milwaukee, oil on cardboard, 15.5×23.5 in., signed, 16.05.2002

To form the interior shape of a casting, a solid sand core is produced, placed into the opened foundry mold, and molten metal is then poured around it. These cores are subsequently destroyed after solidification of the molten metal and after the casting itself is removed for further processing. The first painting illustrates the process of making cores. The coremaker at the center operates a modern high-speed core machine. Silica sand is mixed with chemical binders and blown into a multichambered corebox. The sand mixture is hardened by the introduction of a catalyst. At the end of the cycle, the corebox opens automatically and the finished cores are ejected. They are placed in the fixture of an index table, and the second operator finishes the shaping of the cores.

Tylle, Hans Dieter [German, *1954]: Foundry Bay, ACE/CO,
Milwaukee, oil on canvas, 47×71 in., 2002, signed

The smaller oil study to the right captures the foundry atmosphere to assist the artist as he reconstructs the scene on the much larger canvas above with additional details later in his studio. To the left is a melting furnace with an open well filled with liquid aluminum, a pouring ladle, and a dross pot on its ledge. The lineup of casting machines contains the permanent steel molds. These tilt machines have mounted pouring cups to be filled with molten aluminum by the caster in the foreground. From this filled pouring cup the molten metal enters the mold cavity as the casting machine raises to its vertical position, thereby providing a controlled metal flow to reduce potential turbulence. After the metal solidifies, the mold is brought back into the horizontal position and opened. The hot castings are placed on cooling conveyors for further processing. The caster in the center of the painting dips his ladle into the furnace well, dipping out aluminum to fill the pouring cup for the next cycle. To improve the final composition, Tylle added a second caster to the right of the finished painting. A cooling and straightening fixture is shown to the right. The foundry bay is well lit to allow the caster to see any potential defects. Conveyors transport the castings in the background.

Study to *Foundry Bay*, ACE/CO, Milwaukee,
oil on cardboard, 15.5×23.5 in. signed, 13.05.2002

Tylle, Hans Dieter [German, *1954]: Permanent Mold
Machines, ACE/CO, Milwaukee, oil on canvas, 35.5×59
in., 2002, signed

A smaller subarea of a larger foundry bay is shown
here. The oil study sketch only shows the foundry
environment. Tylle introduced the casting workers
into the final version of his painting. For that purpose Tylle employed a local model wearing ACE/
CO uniforms, hard hats, safety shoes with spats,
gloves and face shields all designed to protect the
working caster from possible metal splashes and
burns.

Study to *Permanent Mold Machines*, ACE/CO, Milwaukee,
oil on cardboard, 15.5×19.5 in., signed, 13.05.2002

Tylle, Hans Dieter [German, *1954]: Aluminum Melting Furnace, ACE/CO, Milwaukee, oil on canvas, 47×71 in., 2002, signed

This oil sketch and large oil painting later finished by H.D. Tylle show two large reverberatory melting furnaces that melt aluminum ingots. Stacks of primary and secondary, or recycled, ingots are shown around the charging wells in the center with additional stacks at the far wall. These ingots are first preheated on the furnace ledge before being lowered into the bath of molten aluminum. The front of the gas-fired furnace is tapped periodically to fill the transfer ladle shown at the right suspended from a hoist on a running track. The transfer ladle then delivers the molten aluminum to the casting station.

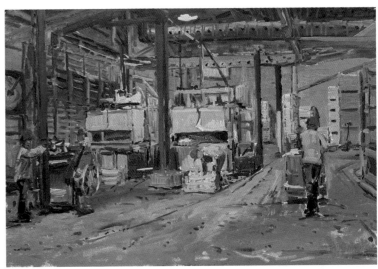

Study to *Aluminum Melting Furnace*, ACE/CO, Milwaukee, oil on cardboard, 15.5×23.5 in., signed, 14.05.2002

Tylle, Hans Dieter [German, *1954]: Aluminum
Molding Line, ACE/CO, Milwaukee, oil on canvas,
23.5×31.5 in., 2003, signed

This painting shows a modern automated vertical molding machine attended by an operator. The chamber in front of the operator contains steel patterns used to produce the molds. The prepared green sand is blown into the chamber between these steel patterns and squeezed to form a green sand mold with the cope and drag impressions on each side. When the door tilts away and the chamber opens, the machine pushes the finished mold onto the molding line. If required for the product, the operator can position one or more sand cores between the two mold halves before closing the sand mold. After the vertical mold is closed, it continues down the line and is subsequently filled with metal, as shown on top of the mold line. That way, 200 to 300 molds per hour can be produced, depending on the casting complexity. The casting solidifies on the mold conveyor and is removed at the end for further processing, while the green sand is recycled. Between the operator and the pouring ladle to the right, we see a conveyor rack bringing sufficient quantities of sand cores from the core room.

Study to *Aluminum Molding Line*, ACE/CO,
Milwaukee, oil on cardboard, 12×15.5 in.,
signed, 14.05.2002

Tylle, Hans Dieter [German, *1954]: Cleaning the Furnace, ACE/CO, Milwaukee, oil on canvas, 35.5×55 in., 2003, signed

The central focus of this painting is an open reverberatory melting furnace. A foundryworker uses a long stoker to loosen the accumulated oxides splashed on the walls of the furnace. The loosened oxides fall into the molten bath, are subsequently skimmed off as dross and sold to a recycler who reclaims the aluminum content. In front of the furnace are a spare furnace door, a drum to hold the dross, and a stack of aluminum ingots to recharge the melting furnace. In the finished painting the artist added a second foundryworker to portray the physical effort of this operation.

Study to *Cleaning the Furnace*, ACE/CO, Milwaukee, oil on cardboard, 15.5×23.5 in., signed, 11.05.2002

Tylle, Hans Dieter [German, *1954]:
Skimming the Dross, ACE/CO,
Milwaukee, oil on canvas, 31.5×39.5 in.,
2003, signed

This additional painting shows two foundryworkers fluxing and cleaning the molten aluminum bath. The skimmed off dross is dipped into the blue drum. Its pure aluminum content is later reclaimed by a recycler and used again.

Tylle, Hans Dieter [German, *1954]: Quenching, oil on canvas, 31.5×23.5 in., 2002, signed

The physical properties of aluminum castings can be improved by heat-treating. The precise treatment depends on the particular aluminum alloy. The castings are placed in a round steel tank and exposed to an 8-10 hour treatment in a round pit furnace at 1000° C. At this temperature the alloying elements (silicon, magnesium, copper, iron, etc.) become evenly distributed throughout the aluminum alloy. To retain this metallurgical structure as the temperature is reduced to room temperature, the steel tank containing the castings is pulled out of the pit furnace with a hand-operated hoist and quickly quenched in warm water. This painting shows the operator, wearing his protective clothing, lowering the castings into the quench water, thereby creating a dramatic cloud of steam. In the foreground is the burn chamber of the heat-treating pit furnace. Beyond the quench water tank is another pit furnace. In the tradition of industrial art, the company owner is shown in the right background.

Tylle, Hans Dieter [German, *1954]: Final Inspection, ACE/CO, Milwaukee, oil on canvas, 35.5×47 in., 2002, signed

This painting presents the last workstation prior to shipping the aluminum castings. Hanging conveyors deliver the castings after removal of the sand cores, removal of the gates and risers, and finishing. Two operators with air tools inspect the parts again very closely and remove minor flash or traces of sand before shipment.

Study to *Final Inspection*, ACE/CO, Milwaukee, oil on cardboard, 15.5×23.5 in., signed, 14.05.2002

Koopmann: Foundryman With Ladle, carved oak, 33 in.

The foundryman by Koopmann is produced of carved oak wood, which is a very unusual medium for this theme. This uniqueness allows the statue to make a very different impression. The artist is not primarily interested in portraying precise reality, but rather in conveying the physical exertion, strength, and concentration required during the metal pouring process.

Anonymous: Foundryworker, cast iron, 19×16 in., ca. 1920

The foundryworker subject of this decorative iron wall plaque casting wears heavy protective work clothes. He holds a sampling ladle with a pouring spout for transferring molten metal into the mold that stands at the base of the ornamental arch.

Elischer, John Wolfgang [Austrian]: Foundryman, cast iron, 16 in., 20th c., signed

Employing a steadied pouring ladle, as illustrated by these two foundrymen, enables accurate control of the process of pouring molten metal. The left worker continues to

Elischer, John Wolfgang [Austrian]: Foundryman, cast iron, 15.25 in., 20th c., signed

pour a steady stream into the mold, but the foundryman on the right appears to be finished. Only slag remnants remain on his ladle.

Müller, H. [German]: Pouring Off, bronze, 11.8 in., signed

The foundryman in this piece is using his enormous casting ladle to pour metal into a box-shaped sand mold.

Lipp, Peter [German, 1902-1975]: Foundryman, cast iron, 9.5 in., Buderus-Kunstguss

Anonymous: Foundryman With Ladle, bronze, 12 in.

Two foundrymen are shown with their pouring ladles. Comparing them employs considerable artistic license to study the difference between the "realistic" portrayal at the left, and the "artistic" portrayal at the right. The left foundryman is equipped with complete protective safety clothing, including gloves. The right worker, however, would in reality burn his right hand and have his unprotected arms at risk. The artist is merely interested in sculpting an athletic male figure.

Anonymous: Foundry Pourer, cast iron, 21 in., Buderus-Kunstguss

In the sculpture above, the worker's right hand is protected against radiant heat with a turned-up mitten. His work clothes, consisting of heavy-duty boots, a pair of leather trousers, a shirt of slightly lighter leather, and a leather helmet, all prepare him for his potentially dangerous job.

Alexander, Malcolm [American]: Pouring Off, bronze, 16.25 in., 1977, Mathews Classic Bronze, Pittsburgh

The foundryman above is pouring molten iron into a hexagonal, three-way parted flask holding a sand mold. In contrast to many other sculptures of the same subject, Malcolm Alexander has chosen to portray a thin, aging, muscular worker who does not personify heroism, but rather reality.

Baumeister-Bühler, Elisabeth [German, *1912]: Foundryman, cast iron, 16 in., Buderus-Kunstguss

This foundryman has a vastly oversized pouring ladle. That fact and his bared upper chest are intended to enhance the decorative value of the sculpture.

**Schaffert, K. [German]: Foundryman With Ladle,
bronze, 13 in., ca. 1900, signed**

The small ladle above is used to sample the quality of the
metal to be cast. After solidification, the metal specimen is
removed from the ladle and examined in the laboratory.

Driesch, Erich van der [German]: Foundryworker, bronze, 25×26×11 in., signed

This foundryman worker performs a symbolic pour. The ladle is fastened to a long handle, permitting a very accurate pour into the mold. The foundryman's safety clothing is exemplary.

Graefner, L. [German]: On the Foundry Floor, bronze, 12 in., signed

With a well-controlled ladle, this foundry caster pours molten metal into a sand mold that is held together with a steel clamp.

Janensch, Gerhard Adolf [German, 1860-1933]: Foundryworker, bronze, 16.5 in., 1916, signed

The worker above is holding a test ladle in his hand. Via such a ladle he removes a liquid specimen material, which he is going to leave in the ladle to solidify. After solidification, the sample will be shaken out of the ladle and examined.

Janensch, Gerhard Adolf [German, 1860-1933]: Foundryworker With Ladle, bronze, 16.5 in., 1918, signed

Here Janensch portrays an idealized foundryworker who steps ahead with a full ladle equipped with a splash shield to protect his left hand. As with many sculptures of workers, the unrealistic bared chest of the statue is intended to give it a heroic male appearance.

Anonymous: Worker With Ladle, cast iron, 18 in., Buderus-Kunstguss

These two cast iron sculptures portray steel foundrymen in their work clothes at the pouring station. They are

Lipp, Peter [German, 1902-1975]: Worker With Ladle, cast iron, 9.5 in., Buderus-Kunstguss

presented in a manner typical of memorials. They exude dignity, intensity and professional pride in their work.

Baumeister-Bühler, Elisabeth [Deutschland, *1912]:
Foundry Group, cast iron, 17.5×25.5 in., 1952, Buderus-Kunstguss

The carrying device above is equipped with a forked handle and a center loop to hold the casting ladle. The transportation and pouring of the molten iron can be handled in a highly practical manner where the forked end controls turning and the other end contributes to lifting. Both workers are wearing caplike protective headgear.

Anonymous: Two Workers Pouring, bronze, 5×9
in., ca. 1900, inscribed "Gelsenkirchener Gußstahl
u Eisenwerke / Vormals Munscheid u Co /
Gelsenkirchen."

Two foundry casters are pouring molten bronze into a
prepared mold. The worker to the right holds the forked
handle of the carrying device in both hands and turns the
pouring ladle slowly towards the viewer. The worker on
the left simply supports a portion of the ladle's weight.

Alexander, Malcolm [American]: First Heat, bronze, 17.5 in., 1978, inscribed "Mathews Classic Bronze, Pittsburgh. ed. 30. Backbone of America Series"

This sculpture shows a medium-sized ladle in the midst of a casting operation. With his available force increased with mechanical devices, the foundryworker is able to tilt the ladle and discharge the molten iron into the runner.

The hand wheel allows the foundryworker to position the ladle horizontally by employing a rack and gear pinion. The ladle is suspended from an overhead crane.

Lamb, Landon [American, born and raised at Yakakima Indian Nation]: Joltin' Joe, bronze, 9×6×8 in., 1985, inscribed "limited ed. of 250, commissioned by Cast Metal Industry (CMI) AFS/CMI"

Joltin' Joe produces a green sand mold in a basic and simple squeeze-molding machine. He manually shovels the green sand into the flask, distributes it with his hands around the pattern, vibrates the flask to uniformly pack the green sand into the mold half, strikes the excess sand off, and squeezes the mold for uniform consistency and hardness. The upper and lower mold halves, called "cope" and "drag," respectively, are assembled into a finished sand mold ready to be poured off. Joltin' Joe was the nickname of a renowned baseball player, Joe DiMaggio, who played around the 1940s. This statue was used by the *American Foundry Society* (AFS) for public relation purposes.

Meissner, Max [*1859]: Foundryman With Ladle, bronze, 12 in., signed

Schiepelkamp: Bell Foundryman, bronze, 22 in., ca. 1920

A foundryman with a ladle and a bell founder are presented at rest. Both wear heavy protective clothing to protect themselves against potential burns. The bell founder proudly presents his finished product. In his right hand

he holds the symbol of his trade guild; this tiny ladle is for dipping samples of the molten bronze metal before pouring.

Forge Shops

Hummel, Theodor [German, 1864-1939]: At the Steam Forge, oil on canvas, 19×23 in., signed

The steam hammer is at its top rest point, ready to start its subsequent descent. The four forge workers are directing the workpiece from in front of the anvil with the help of a pair of spoon-shaped tongs of enormous dimensions.

Another steam hammer is operating at the center of the painting, next to a crane. At the left, another group of forge workers is preparing an additional forging.

**Unknown: Large Hydraulic Forge Press With Workers,
oil on canvas, 39×31 in., signed**

A hydraulic six-post forging press is shown. It is capable of producing a force of up to 30 tons on workpieces. In the operation illustrated in this painting, large blocks formed in the steel mill casting house are initially heated to a glowing state and forged at the ends to form two end supports, or plugs. Each end plug is hung from a chain loop as seen in the painting. Then the rough workpiece between the end plugs is lengthened to a six-sided shaft with continual pressing in the forge, guided by transverse movements of two overhead cranes and the turning of the piece. The turning of the forge piece is accomplished by the chain loop at each end. The worker in the foreground supervises the lengthening process with a measuring stick.

Sandrock, Leonhard [German, 1867-1945]: At the Forge, oil on canvas, 28×35 in., signed

This forging press is capable of producing workpieces ranging from 5 to 15 tons in weight. As graphically illustrated in the painting, this type of press can produce high quality plate-shaped collars and size reductions for future bearing installations. Because the workpieces have such great mass, their slow cooling results in a work cycle of up to one hour in the press. The elevated position of the workpiece is due to a pair of chain loops, whose pulleys are supported by two jib-shaped service cranes. Open-die forged pieces of the kind displayed in this painting are of considerable value.

Nus, Willy: Transporting Large Heated Workpiece, oil on canvas, 31.5×47 in., ca. 1910, signed

A cart riding on rails carries a hexagonal steel beam from inside the preheater unit to arrive at just the right temperature for forging. The rolling cart is pulled as well as pushed. The still open furnace and the workpiece it-self illuminate the three workmen pulling the cart. The workpiece's destination is the steam-powered hammer, seen creating the clouds of steam filling the background of the fabrication bay.

Weil, Chr.: Steel Mill Work at the Forge Hammer, oil
on cardboard, 19×26 in., 1947, signed

The forging press is producing a cylindrical workpiece several meters long. The four-legged easel at the right holds an engineering blueprint. To avoid going out of tolerance, the dimensions of the workpiece need to be checked between each series of forging strokes. Pattern forms that can be placed on the workpiece to check its dimensional accuracy lie next to the crowbars on the floor, in the right foreground. Using this method, the forging press can produce complicated shapes. The bell-shaped structure between the posts is the dome of the hydraulic fluid reservoir. Motors pumping hydraulic fluid drive the forge hammer. The allowable forging time for a workpiece of this size is about one hour. The forging time is limited by the cooling of the workpiece.

Neuerburg, Gerhard [German, 1872-1946]: Large Punch Forge, oil on canvas, 19×23.5 in., signed

In this forge shop, heated metal pieces are placed into the carefully constructed metal cavities of freestanding forge presses, in order to produce the desired shape. At the right stands a preheated oven for heating the forge slugs. In the center stands a hydraulic forging press, and in the background is a friction, or flywheel, press. To the left is a long workbench used to straighten and cut to length the long rolled shapes, and perhaps also to prepare pieces for reheating.

Neuerburg, Gerhard [German, 1872-1946]: Two Forges, oil on canvas, 13.5×21 in., signed

Two kinds of forging equipment are depicted: a steam hammer for forming larger pieces, and two forging hearths. The forging hearths are fired by hard coal and employed as reheating devices for small- and medium-sized workpieces during the forging process. The booms of handling cranes can be seen to the right and left of the steam hammer cylinder. A second steam hammer can only be identified by the booms of its handling cranes. Several workshop anvils dominate the left side of the painting along with appropriate forging tools for detailed forming during the forging process.

SCULPTURES OF BLACKSMITHS AND FORGERS AROUND 1900

Around the beginning of the 20th century, the art world loved symbols and allegories. This was particularly true for sculptures, produced at this time in a wide range of sizes and in great quantities. Thus numerous sculptures exist with the theme of work and industry. These range from small works intended for a living room or office, to bigger-than-life sculptures for public places in cities. A number of sculptors also created memorials to work as sympathetic monuments to the productivity of the nation.

In the ECKHART G. GROHMANN COLLECTION are many examples of such art. Most of these examples portray blacksmiths and foundrymen. This chapter deals particularly with the blacksmith shop, an extraordinary and popular theme. Not only was the blacksmith the subject of thousand-year-old myths, but he was also the accepted symbol of the iron and steel ages. Iron and steel symbolize strength and toughness, as well as the harnessing of fire for human exploitation. The modern defense industry, the dominant force in the age of imperialism, is unthinkable without steel. Therefore, the blacksmith embodies the military strength of the nation in many sculptures. Beyond that, he also symbolizes the heavy physical labor of the male. With this background in mind, repeatedly finding such sculptures to be idealistic and unrealistic is no surprise.

The ECKHART G. GROHMANN COLLECTION includes two kinds of metalworkers. One is the traditional trade worker, the blacksmith, as we saw him in the chapter dealing with preindustrial work. The other is the industrial metalworker, or forger, who labors in the steel mill. Both are shown here because they represent the art of the 19th century and provide a good comparison. Their stylistic forms show very little difference.

Anonymous: Forge Worker With Tongs, cast iron, 19×16 in., ca. 1920

Both rollers of a double roller press are depicted here. The rolling mill worker and his heavy tongs are out of place in this piece. For that reason, this presentation serves more as a wall decoration than anything else.

Seger, Ernst [German, 1868-1939]: Blacksmith With Wheel, bronze, 9.5 in., signed

This piece expresses the allegorical character of metalworking sculptures very clearly. The wheel symbolizes technological creativity and progress. The metalwork reinforces the image, which embodies dynamic posture and evident pride.

Küppers, Albert Hermann [German, *1842]: Blacksmith, bronze, 23.5 in.

The blacksmith above holds a sledgehammer, which rests on his anvil. Leaning against the anvil, is a cutting hammer, whose face reveals strong evidence of wear. For safety reasons the blacksmith wears a leather apron and sturdy footwear, along with a visored cap at his disposal.

Allermann: Forging a Sword, bronze, 10 in., signed "Allermann fec," Foundrymark: "Aktienges. Gerd Drichtshagen, vorm." Lauenberg & Sohn

The 19th-century blacksmith represented, among other things, strength and military power. To underline this interpretation, this blacksmith labors to produce a sword.

Gaudez, Adrien-Etienne [French, 1845-1902]: Forger, bronze, 39.5 in., signed on base "A. Gaudez," inscribed "escutcheon: Forgeron"

This metalsmith is fabricating an annular-shaped neck section of a suit of armour. The set of tongs feature two ring-shaped devices to hold the forging tight.

Gaudez, Adrien-Etienne [French, 1845-1902]: Blacksmith of 16th Century, bronze, 23.5 in., signed "Gaudez Paris," Foundrymark "B. D. Vrai Bronze Paris"

Although created from a 19th-century perspective, this horseshoe blacksmith is actually in a 16th-century setting. This sculpture is typical of the idealistic presentation of the 19th century.

Anonymous: Man With Hammer, bronze, 12.75 in.   **Anonymous: Worker Swinging Hammer, bronze, 10.5 in.**

In contrast with the powerful blacksmiths featured on the previous pages, the four bronze figures here portray rather slim and dynamic men. All have trim and well-developed

bodies and correspond almost perfectly with today's male ideal. The first three appear to effortlessly swing their heavy hammers. The blacksmith at the far right symbol-

Beck, E. [German, 19ᵗʰ c.]: Forger With Hammer, bronze, 18 in., signed

Kowalczewski, P. [German, 1865-1910]: Man With Anvil and Gear, bronze, 8.7 in.

izes Adonis. Beck placed a piece of railroad track at the feet of his blacksmith, clearly depicting the product of his efforts. These sculptors clearly demonstrate the idealism of the blacksmith figure.

**Picault, Emile Louis [French, 1840-1915]: The Forger,
white metal, 29 in., signed**

The four blacksmith figures above each represent a different character type. At the far left, the romantic blacksmith
by Picault is reminiscent of the jungle figure Tarzan. He is

**Cancioni, A. [Italian]: Worker With Hammer, bronze,
21.5 in., 1902, signed**

a genuine man of nature. Next to him, Cancioni's stately,
dignified, walking blacksmith is in the manner of Meunier.
He embodies a contemplative manner.

Schmidt-Felling [German]: Worker, bronze, 4 in., 1900, signed

Schmidt-Felling's figures are typical, idealistic tradespeople that exude professional qualifications. Their pride in their trade stands in stark contrast to the industrial

Schmidt-Felling [German]: Forger Swinging Hammer Onto Workpiece, bronze, 11.5 in., signed

model of mass production. They are symbols of a dying trade.

Meunier, Constantin-Emile [Belgian, 1831-1905]: Master Forger, bronze, 19 in., 1890, signed

Meunier's famous *Marteleur* (hammersmith) leads this array of industrial forge figures. Relaxed and leaning against the pair of large tongs which he uses to pull hot forge pieces out of the oven, this forger appears a self-confident master of his trade.

Picault, Emile Louis [French, 1840-1915]: Le Travail (Work), bronze, 12.5 in., signed

Picault's forger is also presented with his tools. As a stage prop, he holds his tongs in his right hand and has his anvil next to him. A gear lies at his feet as a symbol of the engineer's art.

Anonymous: Forger With Tongs, bronze, 18.5 in., ca. 1900

This sculpture is probably a steel mill worker because his left foot is placed on a metal entry guide, which guides the rolled material into the mill. The worker's headgear and heavy apron, supplemented by firm leather boots with a particularly thick sole, provide a suitable kind of protection against the effects of the heat generated.

Reusch, Johann Friedrich [German, 1843-1906]: Forger, bronze, 14 in., signed "Reusch Königsberg," foundrymark "WMF Geisslingen Stg"

The cube-shaped object between this rolling mill worker's feet represents a billet. In the actual rolling operation, a billet can be up to 10 meters or so in length. Rolling mill workers need to turn such a billet 90 degrees after the billet has left the roller groove.

Anonymous: Forger With Tongs Grabbing Workpiece, bronze, 8 in.

This bronze sculpture portrays a rolling mill worker handling a set of transport tongs. He lines up the end of a run-out billet with the next groove of the roller in preparation for the subsequent rolling pass.

Torf, V.E.: The Steelworker, bronze, 24.5 in., signed

This rolling forge worker's function is to turn billets on edge to allow the rolling reduction of their cross dimension. After turning this piece, he feeds the turned stock at his left foot into the mill stand again to make another pass. This worker wears a leather shirt, a leather apron, and heavy leather boots with thick soles as protection against the heat.

**Scholter, H. [German]: Worker and Boss, bronze, 9 in.,
ca. 1930, signed**

This bronze figure was created as a present to "an old friend" worker for his 60th birthday. This pairing of an engineer or supervisor with a worker is found frequently in pieces from the 1920s and '30s. It symbolizes the cooperation of intellectual and manual labor. The two are not adversaries but rather mutually supportive. The considerable actual difference in status and pay are ideologically downplayed.

**A.T., monogrammed: Forger and Engineer, bronze,
17.25 in., ca. 1920, foundrymark "DEW"**

Here is another variation on the pairing of engineer and worker. The "workers of brain and fist" form a harmonious team for the benefit of the company. One carries the trade implement of large tongs, while the other carries paper documents such as blueprints and calculations.

**Jäger [German]: Blacksmith Apprentice Sitting on
Anvil With Hammer, bronze, 8 in., signed**

At the conclusion of this series of bronze blacksmith statues is a more unusual figure, an apprentice of the blacksmith trade. He has probably just worked with the large sledgehammer and therefore seems exhausted. Nonetheless, he has a determined expression. He wants to learn his trade. "All beginnings are difficult" according to a German saying which is perhaps appropriately expressed by this bronze statue.

Rolling Mills

The ECKHART G. GROHMANN COLLECTION has commissioned a full-sized copy of the famous and very important industrial painting *The Rolling Mill* by Adolph Menzel. The large original painting is in the *National Gallery* collection in Berlin. Because Menzel added a tar material to his paint, his original oil paintings continue to darken and are losing their brilliance. A skillful copy should reproduce the original colors of Menzel's work in a more stable form, while the original will continue to darken.

The Rolling Mill is the first large-scale industrial painting in Germany to focus on the contemporary working process. The painting is a composition of various typical industrial scenes. Menzel spent three years creating *The Rolling Mill* during which he also prepared many detailed drawings at the mill location to better understand and realistically portray the subject matter. During this time he devoted his energy exclusively to this painting. Many of his sketches are still in existence today, providing witness to Menzel's devotion to this project.

Shown here is the rolling mill bay of the steel mill at Königshütte in upper Silesia, a former area of Germany annexed to Poland after World War II. As the most modern plant of its kind in Europe, it was considered a Prussian showcase for over 100 years. This painting symbolizes the industrialization process in at least two ways. First, the steel processing was a key technical driver of the industrial revolution. In addition, the production of steel railroad tracks symbolizes the transformation of natural environment into an industrial landscape.

One could interpret the Menzel painting as a modern version of the traditional theme seen in the *Forge of Vulcan*. It follows the mythologically-oriented tradition of the blacksmith theme and was interpreted in this manner by his contemporaries. At one point, with Menzel's consent, it was named *Modern Cyclopes*. Menzel himself originally called it *Interior of a Steel Mill*.

The glowing iron is the main source of light in the center, and the "Cyclopes" perform their work with physical strength and accumulated knowledge. Menzel himself describes his work as follows:

"The stage is one of the large workshops producing railroad tracks at Königshütte in upper Silesia. Moveable walls are raised up to permit daylight to enter. A long, glowing, white-hot workpiece is ready to be rolled at the first rolling station. The two workers, transporting the hot workpiece on the cart, are now sliding it into the rolling station by lifting wagon handles, while three additional workers are focused on guiding the workpiece with their metal tongs. The workers beyond this work station are ready to receive the workpiece after the first pass through the roller. With tongs and hanging support rods from above, they will repeat the rolling process again and again between rail profile rollers, until the workpiece eventually attains the desired shape for the railroad track. On the left, a worker drags a steel cube forged by the steam hammer to a cooling area. Behind him, in the background, a puddle furnace is attended by workers under the eyes of the managing director ["Dirigent": "conductor"] of the mill. A shift change is approaching: in the left middle, half naked workers are washing up, and to the right workers are eating a hearty lunch brought in a basket by a young girl." [Staatliche Museen zu Berlin (ed.): Adolph Menzel, Berlin 1980, 308 f.].

The managing director, dressed in a suit and hat, is visible far in the left background of the painting, and also in detail at right. By reconstructing the vanishing point of the composition, the director is at eye level in the painting and, without great visibility, still drives the painting's action.

Menzel, Adolph [German, 1815-1905]: The Iron
Rolling Mill, oil on canvas, 62×100 in., 1872/75;
Staatliche Museen zu Berlin - Preußischer Kulturbesitz,
Nationalgalerie

No other painting has had more influence on the next generation of painters, and no other painting has ever been treated as the icon of industrial art. Despite being acknowledged as a masterful painting, *The Iron Rolling Mill* was interpreted in two opposing ways from its very beginning. Some saw it as an expression of the heroic productivity of modern industry. Others viewed it as a critical portrayal of the difficult working and living conditions of the industrial worker, who contributed all his physical strength in return for a meager reward of poor wages. The piece portrays the contradiction of its time. The German industry boomed, but simultaneously violent strikes occurred, even at Kőnigshűtte at the very time Menzel created this painting. In 1875 this painting was sold from the private collection of the banker Adolph von Liebermann to the *National Gallery* in Berlin.

Montan, Anders [Swedish, 1846-1917]: Armor-plate Rolling Mill
Krupp, oil on cardboard, 22.5×17 in., ca. 1893, signed

The *Friedrich Krupp A.G. Steel Company* commissioned six paintings by
Anders Montan for a public relations project. The oil studies shown here
found their way into the ECKHART G. GROHMANN COLLECTION. To the
right is a copy of the picture that appears in a book issued by the *Krupp
Company*. It illustrates the rolling of the massive armor plate for well-
known tanks built before World War I. The rolling master, in the foreground, directs the process.

Jünger, Josef [ca. 1880-1949]: Workers Dragging a Red-Hot Iron Piece (after Arthur Kampf), oil on canvas, 31×23 in., ca. 1920, signed

This painting is a copy of the 1901 original by Arthur Kampf. Kampf created the picture as a detail from a larger fresco entitled *Rolling Mill*. To the right is a reconstruction of the fresco from 1900. Workers pull glowing iron block on a cart to the rolling machine. In many details, this picture draws upon the famous painting *The Iron Rolling Mill* by Adolph Menzel.

Bollhagen, Otto [German, 1861-1924]: At the Rolling Mill, oil on canvas, 26×45 in., signed

Otto Bollhagen is one of the best-known industrial painters of the first two decades of the 20th century. He had a well-established work shop in the city of Bremen and was busy executing commissions from major industrial companies. This painting illustrates the rolling of steel bars within a large steel mill. At the left, large steel bars with a square profile are being rolled. To the right is another rolling line tooled for a different cross-sectional shape. The mill workers guide and operate the mill processes.

West, F. [ca. 1900-1950]: Rolling Mill With Large Gauge Indicator, oil on canvas, 25×30.5 in., signed

A steel rolling mill is pictured here. The large horizontal steel roller exhibits the various sized grooves available for each rolling pass. The steel bar is rolled back and forth through the rolling mill and is transferred to a smaller groove on each successive pass. The worker to the left supervises and controls the process.

Schreiber [German]: Retrieving Hot Workpiece From Furnace, oil on canvas, 24×36 in., 1940, signed

The chain-controlled door stands wide open. Three workmen employ long forge bars in an attempt to pull a block forging out of the forging furnace. The block glows at the rolling temperature. The outline of a flywheel is visible at the upper left of the painting where its axle extends across the top section of the canvas. The flywheel indicates a forge while the other equipment suggests a rolling mill instead. A shovel and a long bar with a loop handle lean against a column.

**Dollinger, Richard [*1871]: Rolling Mill With
Workpieces, oil on canvas, 38.5×46.5 in., 1927, signed**

This painting illustrates the work process in a rolling mill. To the right, the push through preheating ovens. The two rolling presses in the left background are in tandem. A running hoist transports the forge pieces to the next operation. The second roller at the far left is set up to roll steel rods.

**Hamel, Otto [German, 1866-1950]: Rolling Mill Bay
at the Völklingen Steel Mill, Germany, oil on canvas,
18×23.5 in., signed**

A 60-degree rim section of a large flywheel stands at the rear center of this painting. Flywheels serve to absorb and compensate for load surges produced by the rolling process. The mill operations are aligned in a parallel manner at the level of the flywheel axle. To the right of the painting stands the discharge side of the reheat furnaces. Any movement of material off the rolling line is accomplished with the small carts shown in the foreground. The cart in the foreground carries an ingot, which has cooled down and needs to be reheated inside the furnace. The combustion gases leaving the exhaust system are shown on an exaggerated scale.

Neuerburg, Gerhard [German, 1872-1946]: August-Thyssen Steel Works, oil on canvas, 21×27 in., signed

In this area of the *Thyssen Foundry*, the preheating ovens are shown on the left with overhead ventilating ducts to exhaust the oven fumes. The metal plates are manually removed from the ovens and dragged over to the four rolling mills on the right. The steel rollers of all four mills are synchronized, and are driven by a steam engine with a giant flywheel, the rim of which is shown in the center background. To the right is a forge worker folding an additional metal sheet with his wooden safety shoes before forging it to a thinner gauge.

Mercker, Erich [German, 1891-1973]: Sheet Metal
Rolling Mill, Siegerland, Germany, oil on panel, 18×22
in., signed

The two parallel rolling stations have a common drive, probably powered by a steam engine. The thickness setting of the rough rolling operation at the center of the painting is controlled by means of an electric motor. Screwdown spindles at each end of the roller can be coupled via shafting. The second operation to the right shows both screwdown spindles linked via a shafting that can be disengaged. The plates being rough rolled are still at approximately the furnace temperature. The plates at the finishing operation only show a faint red hue, indicating that the processing operation has come to an end. Rolling workers handle the plates with their tongs. Both operations are equipped with sliding feeder ramps to allow for reverse passes.

**Mercker, Erich [German, 1891-1973]: Block Rolling
Mill, oil on canvas, 20×23.5 in., signed**

The width of this rolling mill is probably exaggerated. A hot block is rolled in the center bay. A new piece is underway in the neighboring mill furnace to the right. At the left of the painting, a feeding roller brings the next block for forging.

**Sandvogl: Steel Rolling Mill, oil on canvas, 30×40 in.,
1926, signed**

A crane structure hangs at the left from its crossbeam supports. By means of large red tongs, the crane carries a metal coil freshly out of the reheating furnace. After the initial rolling, the coil requires an intermediate heat treatment to accomplish leveling and uniform heating. This intermediate process occurs in reheating furnaces, located in the right background, where an open furnace door has produced a reflective glow of fire. When the coil reaches the appropriate temperature, the crossbeam crane conveys it from the furnace directly to its appropriate processing and inspection site. Here, in the middle of the painting, a worker checks the plate for flaws and marks any flaws on the plate with oil chalk. Opposite him is another worker with the same task. A third worker with some type of eye protection is checking the width of the plate with a measuring rod. To the left foreground a worker shovels trimmed edge chips into a cart. A white-collar manager is watching the activities at the right center of the painting. He may be an owner, since it was not unusual at this time to illustrate the owner in facility paintings.

Sandvogl: Wide Strip Rolling Bed, oil on canvas, 32×42 in., 1926 (?), signed

This painting depicts the processing of a wide strip of metal plate. Approximately 10 passes reduces the slab to its required thickness, resulting in a considerable lengthening of the rolled stock. The thinner the rolled stock becomes, the faster its cool-down. Taking this into account, thinner plates are processed in an enclosed tunnel to minimize cooling of the rolled stock. Once the ultimate thickness is achieved, the final operation of the last pass is coiling the stock onto a reel. The operator's cabin of the overhead traveling crane is visible above the control panel.

Mercker, Erich [German, 1891-1973]: Sheet Metal
Rolling Mill, Eichen, Germany, oil on canvas,
23.5×31.5 in., 1954, signed

The three rolling mills above have a common driver, probably steam-powered. Each mill consists of two columns, and each column bears a spindle for screwing down the rollers to the correct thickness. At the central unit, the screwdown spindle is activated by a large spoked wheel. The rolling mill worker in the foreground is handling a metal plate about two inches thick, which he has just retrieved from the preheater. He is dragging this plate across square, cast-iron slabs that cover the floor of the rolling workshop. The preheated blank passes through several mill stands and is reduced in thickness each time. On the other side of this trio of mill workers stands a similar set of rolling mill workers who reverse these plates after each pass. The terminal rolling operation is performed on the right at the third mill stand. Two complete and cooled plates already lie in front of this stand.

Anonymous: Steelworker Straightening Hot Plate, oil on cardboard, 18×22 in.

This factory floor is covered with sheet metal plates. The plates are originally cast and then rolled on the flat gauge rolling mill line devices in the background of the paint-ing. During rolling, the plates often are deformed by the heat and subsequently are laid on the flat iron floor to be straightened and adjusted by the workers.

Mercker, Erich [German, 1891-1973]: Brass Rolling Mill, oil on cardboard, 23.5×31.5 in., signed

The operational focus of this painting is a rolling mill stand at the right center. Electric motors are used in a drive system to set correct thickness for this process. A brass strip passes through the rolling operation and a worker is gathering it onto the reel. The mandril at the lower left is the base on which the brass is wound in coils. A large number of brass coils are deposited next to the rolling operation.

A considerably older rolling stand is visible at the far end of the workshop. That unit is used to roll the brass sheets seen between the rolling stands. The spoked wheel sets the roll gap on this older machine. One overhead traveling bridge crane serves both rolling stands. The floor of the rolling mill is clad with square, cast-iron slabs.

METAL PROCESSING

After melting, forging and rolling, the finished metal becomes raw material for the metalworking industry. This is a widely diversified industry which produces a variety of both capital equipment and consumer products. Artists have not found the metal processing industry to be as appealing a theme as mining and ore processing. The spectacles of fire and smoke are diminished in metal processing, providing less drama. The symbolic confrontation between work and the power of nature is also less of a factor.

In spite of this, art history comprises a considerable number of visual pieces featuring the metalworking sector, including examples in the ECKHART G. GROHMANN COLLECTION. These examples range across the spectrum from allegorical works such as the iron bender shown here, to portrayals of grinding and polishing, wire drawing, construction projects, the building of industrial installations, machining and shipbuilding. All these pieces afford a view of the intermediate production and work processes. They combine machines and tools with human effort, mostly performed in large manufacturing plants. The technologies they portray are not always historically accurate, but they generally reflect the working atmosphere of industrial production.

As such, they are not primarily historical technical documents, but rather reflect an artistic impression of the complex system of industrial production, including a sociological view of the work environment in which the workers spend a great deal of their lives.

Müller-Krefeld, Adolf [German, *1863]: Bending Steel Bar, bronze, 28.5 in.

This bender of iron embodies allegorical male power and productivity. This is a typical representation from the period around 1900.

Wahler, Carl [German, 1863-1931]: Boy at Grinding Wheel, oil on canvas, 11×15 in., signed

In the past, a great many workers were needed for grinding activities. The sharpening of swords, scissors, knives and other instruments was a very skilled trade requiring extensive work experience and ability. Thus, the boy shown here probably has a rather simple task, but one that is physically demanding. The grinding wheel is made of sandstone and powered by a water wheel. To ensure a continuous power supply for operation, river dams were erected, providing a sufficient water supply, both in terms of flow volume and pressure.

Anonymous: Knife Grinder, enamel on copper, 7×5 in.

Here is a village grinding scenario, rather than a factory. The grindstone is driven by a foot-powered crank mechanism. The water required for the wet grinding is replenished by the water jug at the base of the grinding tool. The knife grinder wears clogs. The focus of his eyes indicates he is distracted from his grinding activity.

Mercker, Erich [German, 1891-1973]: **Steel Fabrication Bay at Dortmund Union Steel Mill**, oil on canvas, 23.5×31.5 in., 1936, signed

This painting illustrates the production of major girders with websizes exceeding two feet. Such large websizes had to be fabricated by welding metal plates together. The rolled plates used were cut into sheets and strips. As shown in the painting, these components were welded into girders. The white areas that appear at irregular intervals across the painting represent the intense light produced by the flaring of the welding electrodes during the electro-welding process. They cannot fully convey the impression of welding operations being performed in such a large bay. At center left a sheet metal blank is cut by a gas torch before a traveling crane places it at the appropriate assembly position. Several nearby hexagonal blanks are visible. These blanks are cut from plates that are approximately eight inches thick. Later they will be assembled by welding to achieve the desired shapes.

Hayek, Hans [German, 1869-1940]: Ironworks, oil on canvas, 21×25 in., 1915, signed

This painting illustrates the assembly hall of a steel fabrication plant. At the center foreground a railroad turntable assists in the transport of heavy materials. There is little indication of an organized and efficient workflow. The assembly process appears chaotic. This lack of organization may be real or a product of the artist's lack of familiarity with the process. Three workers are shown coping with the situation.

Bindewald, Erwin [German, 1897-1950]: Ball Bearing Press, oil on canvas, 37.5×47 in., 1941, signed, "granted to the departing managing director from the owner Dr. Schäfer, Schweinfurt"

Four ball bearing presses are located in the bay. An electric motor and a belt transmission drive these presses. Each ball bearing press has a flywheel to absorb the impact cycle of the pressing process. There are four oil drip lubricators integrated into the bearing block of the flywheel. The worker in the left foreground is exchanging the receptacle that collects the finished ball bearings. Several coils of wire are placed to the right of the front press. The coils serve as raw material for the ball bearings. The supervisor at left center is adjusting the performance of the press. Safety cages around part of the flywheel are designed to prevent any injuries to the workers. Small trolley cranes help exchange machinery or tools.

Bollhagen, Otto [German, 1861-1924]: Presses for Rivets, oil on canvas, 24.5×41 in., ca. 1910, signed

This rivet press facility fabricates the rivets later used to assemble heavy metal construction frames for bridges and high-rise buildings. The raw material steel plates are preheated at the right and left sides of the painting. Two friction presses, driven by overhead powerbelts, punch the steel plates into rivets. The steam engine in the foreground produces the power for the overhead belt drives.

Röder, Georg [German, *1867]: Ammunitions Factory,
Rheinhausen, oil on cardboard, 23×30.5 in., 1942,
signed

A factory building with skylights contains a considerable number of lathes. The manufacturer of ammunition is not depicted anywhere in the painting, only in its title. The supervisor's office is located in an elevated structure at the left of the picture. This position allows an unimpeded view of the entire workshop. In addition to the turning lathes, several milling machines are visible at the center. Carts are used to transport finished goods and equipment. At the left two men are studying a drawing, while two others at the right confer about a workpiece.

Lova, J. [Austrian]: **Workers in the Hermann Göring Steel Plant, Austria**, oil on cardboard, 27×38 in., ca. 1941-44, signed

A heat treatment oven to prepare long rough iron pieces for further processing is at the center of this picture. With the use of a pair of tongs, a worker loads a wheelbarrow with hot metal parts. These parts supply another worker on the punch press. On the wall at the upper right, an electric motor powers the oven bellows with a drive belt. An exhaust pipe is located above the hood of the oven.

Kley, Heinrich [German, 1863-1945]: Machine Shop
Bay (Overhead Crane and Boring Bar), watercolor on
paper, 15.5×21.5 in., signed

This large manufacturing bay is suited for heavy work-pieces. To the left is a large boring bar. To the right, some-what set back, is a gantry to support boring and milling operations. The base and cover of a turbine housing wait for additional processing. The turbine rotor is located in front of the gantry. Two electric motor starters, one standing and one lying down, are in front of the boring bar. The sturdy construction guarantees the safe transport of heavy loads.

Brosick, Dominik [Austrian, 1873-1935]: Interior of a Stamp Shop, oil on canvas, 31.5×31.5 in., ca. 1930, signed

Three large stamping presses have been set up inside this workshop. In the right-hand corner of the painting is a set of transmission gears containing a large, toothed wheel. A tapered shank, reduced at various points, is suspended down from the hook of a crane. Around the upstairs gallery are smaller stamping machines. A workman is operating one of the stamping machines.

Wever, Heinz [German, 1890-1966]: The Wire Drawing Plant, Silbersiepen, Germany, oil on canvas, 24×32 in., signed

This wire drawing plant is a small business. The conical drums seen throughout the workshop are used to coil the wire during the drawing operation. The finished wire is drawn through a steel die of the desired caliber. Coils of bailing wire hang on the left wall. A kerosene lamp hangs from the ceiling of the workshop and provides some illumination. The operation includes three drawing benches powered by transmission belts connected to the shaft at the ceiling of the bay. There is a wire cutter at the bottom right corner. Beside it are a schnapps bottle, glass and a lunch pail.

Skutezky, Döme [Hungarian, 1848-1921]: Wire Drawing Shop, oil on cardboard, 17×21 in., signed

A gas-fired wire drawing bench stands at the center background of this painting. The drawn wire will be wound onto the reel at the left foreground. The tangle at the left center of the painting probably portrays wound-up wire balls. At right is a furnace for preheating the metal ingots.

Werner, Rudolf G. [German, 1893-1957]: Tapping the Crucible, oil on canvas, 20×28 in., signed

This painting shows a group of workers attending an aluminum crucible melt furnace. Several pouring ladles are ready to be filled with metal. They are held with forked ladle handles. The worker to the left rests on the iron handle of a skimmer used for the removal of oxides and other impurities floating on the surface of the melt, in much the same way as slag on the ferrous melt. He observes the tapping very attentively. The workers in the back wait to receive metal into their designated pouring ladles, and then will pour the metal into molds.

Krug, Karl [*1900]: View of Rosswein's Metalworking Plant, Leipzig, Germany, oil on canvas, 31.5×47 in.

Crucible melting furnaces are located at the right side of this brassworking factory bay. Above the furnaces a system of exhaust ducts removes the poisonous fumes. Scrap metal to be recycled lies in front of the furnace. The control panels needed to monitor the operation of the crucible furnaces are located along the back wall of the building. Despite the exhaust system, the bay is filled with fumes. To the left side of this foundry bay, steel molds are ready for the next charge of molten brass.

Mercker, Erich [German, 1891-1973]: Turbine
Assembly, MAN Nuremberg, Germany, oil and pastel
on board, 15×19 in., signed

The right section of this painting shows two gantries for drilling and milling operations. The left section of the painting is dominated by a single large drilling and milling machine. The workshop provides two tracks for traveling cranes. This double design enables execution of difficult craning operations. The castings are delivered to the manufacturing bay and the sections to be machined are marked with chalk. A turbine housing is located in front of the central gantry, at the left center of the picture.

Mercker, Erich [German, 1891-1973]: Diesel Engine
Test Stand, oil on canvas, 31.5×23.5 in., 1969, signed

This scene probably portrays the diesel engine testing bay at the *Maschinenfabrik Augsburg – Nuremberg (MAN)* facility. Test devices can have dimensions ranging up to three stories high and are located at the center of the painting. In the right foreground is a smaller moveable test stand. A ship's diesel engine block is shown along the left edge of the picture. Three overhead traveling bridge cranes are used inside this workshop. Major diesel units tested here are employed as drive units in ships or stationary power plants.

Unknown: Kettle Maker, oil on canvas, 37.4×31.5 in., ca. 1880, signed

This painting shows the interior of a metal spinning shop. The metal spinner produces a great variety of containers out of soft sheet metal, traditionally tin. Eating and drinking utensils manufactured of tin were in wide use for many years. A piece of the sheet metal is clamped to a lathe. As it spins, the worker forces the sheet metal to assume the desired shape by using the tool visible in his hand, sometimes over wooden patterns.

Stelzer, W.: Fabrication of Pressure Vessels, oil on canvas, 17×20 in., ca. 1940, signed

Vessels of the size shown here require a wall thickness between 5 and 50 mm, which requires a heavy gauge rolled plate raw material. The accurately precut steel plate is formed into the desired shape by heavy-duty bending machines. The correctly shaped parts were then assembled with rivets. Today these assemblies are usually welded. Due to the large area required, the final assembly is often performed outdoors.

Rasmussen, Hans [*1888]: Kalundborg Shipyard, oil on canvas, 23×27 in., 1918, mongrammed "JR"

Shipbuilding is a popular artistic theme. The vertical and horizontal scaffolding structures in shipyards can be as interesting as their enormously large products. The scale of this effort can make the workers appear like ants.

Rasmussen shows a shipyard in sunlight with several iron ships under construction. The rough construction work is finished. Apparently these are a series of sister ships.

Dithmer, Mogens [Danish, *1928]: A Cargo Ship Inside a Dry Dock, oil on canvas, 19×23 in., signed

The cargo ship is placed in a floating dry dock to undergo repair operations, and probably to get a new coating on its hull. The dry dock is initially submerged to allow the ship to enter, and then the water is pumped out of its hollow interior, allowing it to float with the ship aboard. The ship is equipped with twin propellers. Cranes are available to perform various functions on the ship's deck, as well as inside the hull. Once these activities have been completed, the floating dock interior will be flooded, allowing it to descend so that the cargo ship will float again. Generally the crew will stay on board the vessel, particularly since the operations are usually performed within a few days.

Mercker, Erich [German, 1891-1973]: Hamburg,
Blohm und Voss, U-Boat Shipyard, oil on canvas,
39×47 in., 1944, signed

Two almost completed submarines are moored inside the dockyard. Protective awnings cover both submarines to facilitate the installation of the equipment. Another submarine is located on the right. In the background, a new, larger submarine is under construction along the building berth. The dockyard employs a variety of cranes. The funnels of major cargo vessels can be seen in the far background.

Tylle, Hans Dieter [German, *1954]: Norwegian Dawn, Meyer-Werft, Shipyard, oil on canvas, 47×71 in., 2002, signed

Hans Dieter Tylle painted a series of paintings of the *Meyer-Werft* shipyard at Papenburg, in northern Germany. This is a modern, highly mechanized shipyard, utilizing leading edge technology such as laser cutting, computer controlled production methods, and a high degree of automation. The shipyard is located inland on the small and shallow River Ems. Each time a large vessel is completed it must be maneuvered very carefully to the North Sea, creating a major event and great excitement for the local population. This painting shows the construction of the vessel *Norwegian Dawn*, the largest passenger ship ever built in Germany. The luxury liner was built for the *Norwegian Cruise Line*.

Study to *Norwegian Dawn*, oil on cardboard, 15.5×23.5 in., 25.03.2002

Xylander, Wilhelm Ferdinand [Danish, 1840-1913]:
Riveting at the Ship's Hull, Copenhagen, Denmark, oil
on canvas, 21×26 in., signed

A ship supported by wooden ties is under repair, probably in a dry dock. The replacement of a number of steel plates is underway. The plates are lined up on the floor. The box a yard worker carries on his back in the foreground is probably full of hot rivets. The worker to the right swings a sledgehammer. Wooden tie bars support the hull, while several workers sit underneath in front of fires to keep the iron rivets red hot. Since the placement of the new plates takes some time, the rivet fires also support another riveting station, probably further underneath the ship's hull. The outer main plates are fitted first, and the rivet holes are marked to be drilled later in the workshop. After that, the plates are returned to the ship and the final assembly proceeds. [Thanks to Lars U. Scholl, *Deutsches Schiffahrtsmuseum*, Bremerhaven]

Schlageter, Karl [Swiss, *1894]: **Worker With Sweatband
at the Stamping Press**, oil on cardboard, 29.5×37 in.,
1934, signed

This stamping press may use hot or cold workpieces. The leveraged activating rods multiply manyfold the physical strength of the operator. For safety reasons, the press must be operated with both hands.

Industrial Landscapes

Landscapes are the human environment. Landscape painting deals primarily with the relationship between nature and its continual reshaping by humans. Over the course of thousands of years, the natural landscape was adapted and altered in many ways by the demands of agricultural and industrial activities. The development of industry encouraged artists to paint industrial installations in the context of landscapes. Over the past 400 years, the treatment of this subject evolved from the original portrayal of industry as part of the landscapes to separate and distinct industrial landscapes. To some extent the artist seeks to portray a specific industrial installation, but in a more general sense, the objective is to produce a picturesque impression of an industrial district. The result is a spectrum of paintings with themes ranging from the glorification of the industrial age to the critical examination of industrial dominance.

Behrens: Industrial Plant, oil on canvas, 30.5×38 in., 1947, signed

A very compacted presentation of a large factory complex with rail sidings is placed between a blue sky and a golden cornfield. The painter creates a pleasant atmosphere. Agriculture and industry form the basis of prosperity and coexist harmoniously in this world. Created only shortly after World War II, this painting was intended to spread hope and optimism. As smokestacks spew smoke, they symbolize the prosperous future yet to come. They are not allowed to darken the bright blue sky.

Mercker, Erich [German, 1891-1973]: Evening at the Steel Mill, oil on cardboard, 17.5×23 in., 1920, signed

The artistic portrayal in this painting displays a lavish conglomeration of items. Skips, ladle cars and a steam engine are all visible. A red tail lamp is mounted onto the locomotive. Between the engine and the railroad cars a shunter is operating, moving two lamps. Behind them, a casting bay becomes visible with the pig iron about to cool down. There are a number of gas lamps, behind which a rolling mill workshop can be perceived featuring heated-up materials. A tower with a winch house attached, the contours of several recuperators, and structural sections of blast furnaces can be discerned as well.

**Gärtner, Fritz [German, 1882-1958]: Bread and Iron,
oil on canvas, 29×43 in., signed**

Both allegorical paintings by Fritz Gärtner reflect a cultural view common in the period between 1900 and 1945. Agriculture and iron production are combined in the same scene to emphasize both sources of national wealth. Implicit in the scene is mining, which makes the production possible. Gärtner's style yields an idealized and romanticized picture. A grain field in the foreground has been harvested and the sheaves set up to form stock. The industrial complex looms in the background along the banks of a river. A bridge, heavy with traffic, spans the river symbolizing triumph over nature. From the right bank of the river a new expressway bridge is under construction,

Gärtner, Fritz [German, 1882-1958]: Fire and Grain Sheaves, oil on cardboard, 27.5×39 in., 1914, signed

its cantilever projecting over the water. Two blast furnaces at the center release a fiery glow and a pair of recuperators occupies the right side. A forest of smoke stacks dominates the entire scene, the resulting fumes nearly eclipsing the sun. The right painting stresses a romantic view through its nocturnal version with a combination of royal blue and gold colors. It also emphasizes the unceasing power of production, in contrast to the interrupted farming in the foreground.

Korthaus, Carl A. [1879-1956]: Industrial Country, oil on cardboard, 15×19 in., 1925, signed

Here the artist is not pursuing a precise technical rendering of a particular industrial complex, but rather a loose rendering of the visual and emotional impression left by industrial production. He deals with light, shadows and colors in an impressionistic way. The individual buildings and the technical installations meld into a single, large, powerful complex, leaving no room for nature and crowding out the sky.

Mercker, Erich [German, 1891-1973]:
Gutehoffnungshütte Steel Works Oberhausen, oil on
academy board, 15×19 in., signed

A slag heap, planted with grass and shrubs along pathways, dominates the foreground. At center is a row of four operating blast furnaces with additional blast furnaces in the background. The dome-shaped air preheaters are shown near the blast furnaces they serve. The large structure at the center is the steel casting bay for this Siemens-Martin steel plant. A water tower to build pressure is at the left and a cooling tower for water vapor is to the far right.

Kreibich, Oskar [1916-1984]: River Harbor at Heilbronn, Germany, oil on canvas, 50×65 in., 1950, signed

Here is a portion of the important Heilbronn harbor on the Neckar River in southwest Germany. This industrial city, mostly destroyed in World War II, not only rebuilt its industrial base but simultaneously expanded its river harbor to accommodate even larger barges. Loading cranes, industrial facilities, barges and the river are integrated by the painter into a composition extolling the achievements of postwar reconstruction in Germany. The barge in the foreground is a typical river barge loaded with raw materials.

Kortengräber, H. [German]: German Industrial Harbor in Front of Power Plant, oil on cardboard, 27×40 in., 1952, signed

This painting presents a typical view of an industrial river harbor. Large barges are loaded and unloaded by a heavy crane. A group of industrial plants is visible in the background, very close to the harbor. These plants are dependent on low-cost water transport for their raw materials and finished goods. The artist immerses the entire scene in a feathery light and plays with the reflected light from the water's surface.

**Kortengräber, H. [German]: Thyssen's Meiderich Steel
Works by Night, oil on cardboard, 42×58.5 in., signed**

Kortengräber paints the huge *Thyssen* steel mill complex at Duisburg-Meiderich north of Cologne on the Rhine River in Germany. On the left are the air preheaters with the distinctive hemispherical tops; the blast furnaces occupy the center of the painting. The tapping of the blast furnaces to remove the molten metal takes place in the bright area in the exact middle of the picture. The artist's choice of a night setting greatly dramatizes the effect of the bright molten steel. Another visual advantage comes from the double reflection of the bright light from the water, as well as from the smoke and vapor clouds. Both contribute to the very dramatic atmosphere.

Gärtner, Fritz [German, 1882-1958]: Harbor for Shipping Ore, oil on fiberboard, 27×38.5 in., ca. 1920, signed

A great deal of the iron ore needed for the high steel production levels in Germany had to be imported from abroad. Large ocean freighters brought ore to the German seaports. There it was reloaded onto smaller river cargo barges, for delivery to the steel mills located on navigable rivers and canals. Gärtner shows a harbor with large in-transit piles of iron ore. Large bridge cranes transfer the ore to and from these piles. The entire harbor area, as well as the barges themselves, are covered with reddish-brown iron oxide ore dust.

Mercker, Erich [German, 1891-1973]: Copper Mill
at Duisburg on Rhine River, oil on canvas, 40×59 in.,
signed

This painting portrays a bend of the Rhine River in the area of Düsseldorf and Duisburg. There are several steel mills and blast furnaces located on both sides of the river. Along the river, bulk goods are carried in vessels of different types and sizes. There is an abundant array of jibs, cranes and derricks for all sorts of loading and unloading operations. In the middle of the river is a chain of cargo barges towed by a steam tug. Other barges are moored along the banks of the river. The fiery red glow at the center of the painting results from tapping off the pig iron inside a roofed manufacturing bay of a blast furnace. The slagging is performed to the left and to the right of the blast furnace. A chain of four blast furnaces is shown on the far left in front of a line of recuperators. The steam clouds, brightly lit from below, originate from the discharging and quenching of a coke plant. The right side of the painting displays a panoramic view of blast furnaces in operation.

**Perfall, Erich von [German, 1882-1961]: Ships in Front
of Copper Mill, Duisburg, Germany, oil on canvas,
30.5×30.5 in., signed**

Perfall chose a perspective different from Mercker's for his portrayal of the Rhine River and the copper mill in Duisburg. His distinctly horizontal composition divides into three levels: the river, the pier installation, and the apparently monumental blast furnaces. Slag piles, still burning and smoking, are stored on the pier. The ships, moving in the foreground, are cut off by the painter. This technique creates the impression of especially busy barge traffic.

Mercker, Erich [German, 1891-1973]: Steel Industry on Rhine River, Germany, oil on canvas, 23.5×31.5 in., 1966, signed

This scene shows a typical panorama in the Ruhr Valley. A caravan of barges cruises upstream on the Rhine River. In front of the five huffing cranes are a number of cargo ships, moored and ready to be unloaded. The bright light reflected to the right of center originates from an oxygen blast operation inside a steel making plant. At the center, a tapping operation has just taken place in a foundry. To the left are jibs of the inclined skip hoists with hot steam being discharged behind them, most likely from a power plant. To the left, flares from the bleeding of blast furnace top gas are seen burning in the distance. Several recuperators are visible along the left edge of the painting.

Zachau, Willy [1895-1980]: Schwelgern-Harbor in Duisburg, Germany, oil on canvas, 40×47 in., signed

Willy Zachau also chose to paint a view of the large Duisburg industrial harbor complex in the middle of the 20th century. The barge traffic is very heavy. Both sides of the river exhibit storage and handling facilities for raw materials, especially iron ore, and for the slag byproduct generated in large quantities by the steel making process. The steel plants appear far in the background, engulfed in smoke and the glow of fire.

Mercker, Erich [German, 1891-1973]: Industry Harbor,
Hamborn, Germany, oil on canvas, 23.5×31.5 in., 1966,
signed

Hamborn is part of the industrial metropolis of Duisburg. Mercker composed a typical impression of the Ruhr Valley in the 1960s from its component parts: a steel mill, and an iron ore storage facility, as well as the river and the essential barges. With rough, heavy strokes he deposited the oil paint in a strong manner that increased the impressionistic effect. Today's steel industry does not play the same important role of yesterday, and fundamental change has occurred in the industry.

**Mercker, Erich [German, 1891-1973]: Hamburg
Harbor, oil on canvas, 23.5×31.5 in., 1963, signed**

Here is a typical Hamburg Harbor basin. To the left are tripod derrick cranes, supported by two movable legs along the edge of the dock and a third leg toward the cargo shed behind them. The cargo ships are moored along the side of the dock. In the foreground is a tugboat used for turning and towing large vessels. A small launch passes in front of a large bulk carrier. In the right background, a tugboat tows a freighter to the cargo sheds in the distance.

2. Quarries

Stone quarry work has inspired artists repeatedly over the centuries. The selected pieces in the Eckhart G. Grohmann Collection emphasize two particular aspects of stone quarry work for artistic interpretation. On the one hand, the pieces present the geological structures of open soil and stone layers in unusual, and therefore picturesque, views. On the other hand, the hard quarry work inspired artists to choose it as a symbol of extreme human labor. The pieces also play a symbolic, contrasting role: they present the workers as they ready large and heavy sandstone, granite and marble blocks for edifices of the rich and powerful.

Hoffmann, Otto [German, 1885-1915]: Moving the Stone, bronze, 12.5 in., signed

Hoffmann's sculpture represents an allegory typical of the period around 1900. A man attempts to move an extremely heavy stone. The figure embodies the plight of man: to endure his existence through hard work. Of course the effort is neverending. The same subject is at the core of the Greek myth of Sisyphus. Sisyphus must move heavy marble blocks up a mountain only to have them roll back down again, destined to repeat the process. Thus the statue above could reasonably be entitled "Sisyphus."

Bürkel, Heinrich [German, 1802-1869]: Quarry in the Mountains With Farrier, oil on canvas, 17×21 in., ca. 1864, signed

As a painter of the German Romantic period, Bürkel created a variety of paintings depicting farmers, blacksmiths and lime kilns. In this picture he combines quarry and stone cutters with his favorite subject, the horseshoe blacksmith, or farrier. At the left the cutters break out stone, and to the right they shape the stone into blocks for building construction. A stone-milling wheel is also available. An oxen-drawn cart provides transportation into the valley. In the grotto a blacksmith sharpens iron tools and forms horseshoes for the draw horses.

Mercker, Erich [German, 1891-1973]: Stone Quarry, oil on academy board, 15×19 in., signed

Due to geological changes, a formerly flat lake bed is now sloped, an advantage for the quarrying operation. Quarrymen begin work on the rock face at its bottom. They separate the stone by drilling and wedging, and the stone blocks slide down the inclined face. The quarrymen are climbing on the large blocks using ladders as they split the rock by driving steel wedges. Finished stones, completely dressed, are in the right foreground.

Mercker, Erich [German, 1891-1973]: Stone Quarry, oil on academy board, 19.5×23.5 in., signed

This painting depicts a large quarry operation, including a field railroad. The varied colors of the rock strata produce a rather striking feature. Quarrymen are at work dressing large stones in the foreground, diminished by the imposing scale of the operation. The workers live in site camps at the center of the painting. Several steam-powered excavators are operating in the right background.

Mercker, Erich [German, 1891-1973]: Marble for Chancellory, Berlin, Germany, oil on cardboard, 23×27 in., 1940, signed

This painting presents a marble quarry at Dietz on the Lahn River in Germany. Quarryworkers break the marble out of the hillside in large pieces. They shape the rough pieces into square blocks and transport. The marble quarried here was bound for the Chancellory in Berlin, the seat of power for the *Third Reich*. Although many laborers are present here, the workers' activities are not the main subject of the painting. The focus is on the geological structure the quarrying activity has exposed. In the sunlight the white marble layer is clearly discernible from the other stone formation.

Sprick, Richard [German, 1901-1968]: Quarry of Hermann Göring Works, Austria, oil on canvas, 42×54 in., signed

This picture shows how highly fractured stone can be removed simply with a shovel bucket excavator. Thus, viewers might not recognize this as quarrying activity. A field railroad transports excavated materials. The quarryman in the left foreground is secured by a rope to another worker. Additional quarry workers are active in the center. Railroad tracks and transport cars are available at the right. Hermann Göring, after whom the quarry was named, was marshal of Hitler's *Third Reich* regime in Germany.

**Anonymous [French]: Lifting Wheels Above
Underground Quarries Below Paris, oil on canvas,
23×38.5 in., before 1880**

The pictures on these pages illustrate stone quarrying activities assisted by a special device, a large-diameter wood-
en wheel designed to gain mechanical advantage and allow
very heavy stones to be raised. These wheels were especially
important to underground production of limestone blocks
for the building of various structures. The large wheels
were driven either by human workers, as treadmills, or by
animal power, and were widely used in the underground
quarries on the Seine River south of Paris. As seen in the
painting above, these wheels dominated the landscape well
into the 19th century. The schematic drawing to the right,
from the year 1702, illustrates the operation of the wheel.
The quarrying process resulted in large caves later used for
various purposes, including wine storage.

The left painting depicts a dramatic French landscape
punctuated with stone quarries. A large quantity of stone

Vershuur, Wouter [Dutch, 1812-1874]: Quarry, oil on canvas, 53×66 in.

has already been raised. These stones are transported by carriage on a deeply furrowed dirt road. The Vershuur painting on the right is a closer view of a loading station. Here the stone blocks are larger and metal plates reinforce the wagon wheels. The picturesque red loading wheel dominates the scene. In the foreground workers have finished loading a single-axle cart with heavy stone blocks. Because of the heavy load, single axle and the poor roads, the cart's wheels are reinforced with wide metal plates. The road is inclined slightly from the right to left. The lead horse is trying mightily to hold back the heavy wagon. Two additional horses secured to the back of the wagon provide some help. The extraordinary hardship of quarrying work stands in direct contrast to the picturesque execution of the painting.

Nakken, Willem Karel [Dutch, 1835-1926]: At the Quarry, oil on canvas, 29.75×45 in., 1871, signed

This painting by Nakken shows an underground stone quarry from an interesting perspective. The lifting treadle wheel is clearly seen to the left of the painting. A person would climb on the pegs to raise the stone blocks. A single-axle cart with a team of five horses is being loaded with blocks of stone. The cart transports the very heavy load to the stone processing plant where the blocks are cut into appropriate sizes for building construction. The better quality pieces are further processed by stonecutters for use as monuments or major architectural features. The Dutch painter immerses the scene in a mild and warm sunlight to soften the harshness and toughness of the quarry work.

Anonymous, after Friedrich von Keller: Wedge and Boulder, oil on canvas, 28×37 in.

This picture is fashioned after a stoneworker painting by Friedrich von Keller. It faithfully reproduces the dynamic structure of the original work. Workers move a huge rock onto a wooden slide with nothing more than direct and leveraged muscle power.

**Keller, Friedrich von [German, 1840-1914]: Quarry
Worker, oil on canvas, 16×12 in., signed**

Friedrich von Keller's favorite subjects were stone quarry workers and blacksmiths. In discussing his "Worker" painting Keller explained, "I am interested in workers and I enjoy portraying their power and energy." At the time Keller completed this painting in the 1870s, such themes were still unusual and generally held in low esteem by the art world. In this painting Keller created an impressive study of the heavy laborer in a stone quarry. He values the effort of the workers without making them heroes.

Sterl, Robert [German, 1867-1932]: Quarry Worker, oil on cardboard, 12×9 in., 1909, signed

About a generation after Friedrich von Keller, Robert Sterl produced many paintings depicting quarry workers. He discovered the subjects for his paintings and drawings in the Saxon area of the Elbe River. This study shows masons dressing quarry stones recently separated from their natural source. For better access to the stones the masons have constructed a wooden working platform.

Braith, Anton [German, 1836-1905]: Transport of Marble Blocks From Stone Quarries, Carrara, Italy, oil on canvas, 20×32 in., ca. 1900, signed

Ten oxen pull a very heavy block of marble while mules off to the right observe their progress. Each pair of oxen is held apart by means of a crossbar which also serves as a seat for the drivers. Braith's success at portraying this scene of extraordinarily heavy transport is impressive. The white marble shines as a beacon in direct contrast to the almost black oxen. The great expenditure of energy is emphasized by a seeming explosion of stone in the upper left corner of the painting.

**Nerly, Friedrich, the Younger [Italian, 1842-1919]:
Transporting Marble to the Sculptor Thorwaldsen to
Rome, oil on canvas, 31×43 in., signed**

Six yoked oxen are pulling a large block of marble. The
animals seem to have reached the limit of their strength
and are spurred on with pointed poles. The central pair has
already sunk to its knees. A thunderstorm is approaching,
providing additional incentive to hurry. Another wagon
follows in the background. In art history, the approaching
threat of thunderstorms is a favorite vehicle for dramatic
effect, especially in harvest scenes. This stone is bound for
Bertel Thorwaldsen, a famous classic sculptor of the period around 1800.

**Fischer-Cörlin, Ernst Albert [German, *1853]: Digger,
oil on cardboard, 17.5×11.5 in., signed**

This study does not clearly express exactly what the worker is trying to accomplish. He does not appear to be a stonebreaker, but rather appears to be looking for something in the soil, perhaps minerals or even gold. He hoes the gravel carefully with very little effort. The barrel in the background probably serves to collect his findings and holds his tools as well.

Luchhardt, Karl [German, 1886-1970]: Four Horse Hitch Pulling Rocks, oil on canvas, 31×59 in., signed

A wagon greatly overloaded with rough stone blocks is pulled up an incline by a team of four horses. The route leads from the quarry to the stone cutter, who will prepare building blocks. A picturesque mountain panorama is the artist's choice of frame for this image of hard work. Its beauty certainly is appreciated more by the observer than the participants.

Noerr, Julius [German, 1827-1879]: In the Quarry, oil on canvas, 12.5×19.5 in., 1868, signed

Smoke, light and shadow provide a romantic atmosphere to a group of quarry workers taking a break from their efforts. Two laborers join the gathering from the left rear, while still further in the background three workers continue their labors. Even the horses enjoy a respite from their heavy work. The workers have built a makeshift shack for their tools and for protection against stormy weather. Julius Noerr has created an early example of social realism.

**T.L., monogrammed: Marble Cutting With Wire Saw,
oil on canvas, 12.5×23.5 in., 1842**

This oil study, probably originating in Belgium, shows a wire saw cutting marble slabs from large blocks. Two such blocks are strapped in place on the saw bed while an additional block is moved toward the workstation. At the left, a new load of marble blocks arrives on a wagon. Such large stone saws, constructed of wooden beams, have existed since the Stone Age.

Verschneider, Jean [1872-1943]: Stone Breaker, bronze, 38 in.

Verschneider's *Stone Breaker* also has a symbolic meaning. The figure personifies the great effort required of mankind to obtain raw materials from nature. The worker tries to split apart a large rock with a heavy iron rod. As with all sculptures of this kind, one can assume the artist's motive was primarily to depict extreme bodily movements, as well as to exhibit anatomical structure.

3. Glass and Ceramics

In principle, the raw materials for the production of glass and ceramics are very simple: silica sand and other additives, primarily clay and aluminum. These raw materials are plentiful and can be easily mined in natural form in large quantities. Clay vessels date back over 17,000 years. Glass products are known to exist since 4000 B.C. Clay can be easily processed, and simply drying clay results in a hard, brittle state. Depending on the type of ceramics, extreme hardness is a result of heating to temperatures reaching 2000° C.

The basic device for the production of glass is a melting furnace. A furnace of quality construction is absolutely essential. Glass production requires temperatures up to 1600° C depending on the additives employed. Glass crystal requires the addition of metals, such as lead, which results in highly regarded lead crystal.

The high temperature glazing process was well understood in the Far East long before it was introduced to Europe in the middle ages and widely used thereafter. Practically all cultures in human history understood and used ceramics. Ceramic and glass containers served not only pragmatic purposes, but also provided a medium for artistic expression on articles for everyday use.

Unknown: Glass Blower, bronze, 19 in., 1927, monogrammed

By means of his long blowing pipe, this glass blower has withdrawn a mass of hot liquid glass. He places the glass mass from the furnace into a prepared mold and blows into the center of the glass, causing it to expand against the mold and assume that shape. The statue achieves its objective of showing the concentration required of this worker.

Scheckenbach-Leyk: Glass-Works, Willenberg, East-Prussia, oil on canvas, 59×85 in., 1920, signed

This painting shows an economically successful glass factory. On a beautiful summer day the high chimney belches smoke – a popular symbol for economic prosperity. At center of the painting stands a stable containing five carriages, an indication of the factory's production. A pile of what appears to be soft coal, a fuel to heat the glass furnaces, sits in front of the stable. The stately yellow house is probably the owner's residence.

**Zeller, Magnus [German, 1888-1972]: Interiors of
Glass Works, oil on canvas, 39×36, 1945/50, signed**

Zeller illustrates the interior of a glass blowing factory. A large group of glass blowers are shown at their strenuous trade of blowing glass bottles. The workers at the left of the back row create the approximate shape. Workers at the center finish the bottles employing various ingredients to produce density, color, and surface effects. This is not an artistic workshop but rather a facility for mass production. At the lower right, a woman loads a basket filled with finished products. The woman behind her holds a glass jar at the end of an iron rod. She will transport the hot jar to the cooling oven. A truck waits outside the shop to transport the glassware. Zeller portrays the working atmosphere extremely well in this intensive painting. [Thanks to Michael Funk, *Westfälisches Industriemuseum* (Westphalian Industrial History Museum)]

Firmin-Girard, Marie François [French, 1838-1921]: The
Glass Blowers in Incheville, oil on canvas, 32.5×46 in.,
signed

Both paintings on this double page illustrate the interior of a large French glass manufacturer in the period around 1900. At the center of the left painting stands a large melting furnace. Here a mixture of approximately three-fourths quartz with various other additives is raised to a temperature of 1500° C and melted into a homogeneous liquid mass. At subsequent workstations, the hot liquid is formed into desired shapes and products by long blow-pipes and other tools. Additional ovens are provided to reheat the molten glass for additional forming. Finished

**Firmin-Girard, Marie François [French, 1838-1921]: Glass
Blowers, oil on panel, 15×10 in., signed and dedicated "a mon ami le
Docteur Pozzi, Firmin-Girard"**

pieces are placed into the baskets in the foreground – hot pieces to the right, cooled pieces to the left. The painting to the right depicts the blowing of glass in greater detail. An apprentice holds the prefabricated mold into which the glass expands when the worker blows into its center.

The heat and effort of blowing places a great strain on the lungs and ultimately wears out the glass blower. The trade of glass blowing requires great skill and in early times was passed on only from father to son.

Villemsens, Jean Blaise [French, 1806-1859]: Firing Ceramic Wares, oil on canvas, 20×24 in., 1842, signed

This substantial furnace is decorated with structural components reflecting classical designs. The casting process is in full operation. The combustion chambers are charged with bundles of brushwood, which are dragged from their position in the foreground to the opening of the furnace. Brushwood provides a high rate of energy production but does not last long. The men in the foreground do not seem to be members of the working staff.

**Mogk, Johannes [1868-1921]: Glass Cutter's Workshop,
oil on canvas, 20.5×25.5 in., 1916, signed**

The rough products of the glass blowing operation are ground and polished to yield their desired final appearance. This glass grinder uses a hand grinding wheel, probably driven by an electric motor. The finishing decoration follows prescribed patterns, strongly influenced by fashion trends, while also relying on designs identified with the particular glass factory. This function must be executed with utmost care to avoid creating scratches and to also avoid inhaling the silica dust. The artist depicts the relaxed professionalism of a master.

Scholten, H.K.F.: At the Pottery, oil on canvas, 23×20
in., ca. 1930, signed

The potter's wheel has existed for more than 6,000 years. Whether with the original foot power or with today's electric motor, a flat round turntable is set into motion. Various shapes can be created by hand from a prepared clay mass, particularly hollow jars, as illustrated in this painting. After producing the desired shape the jars are put off to the side for air-drying. A glazing compound may then be applied, followed by baking at high temperatures in a glazing oven. The ceramic wares must be made with great care to avoid cracking during the high-temperature firing process in the curing oven.

4. Construction

The available images of construction activity in the history of work generally are not intended simply as documentation of how construction was performed. More often these images have a symbolic and allegorical purpose. One of the most famous construction projects, the *Tower of Babel* (Genesis 11:1-9) story from the Bible, was an extensively used subject in middle ages, particularly in the 16th and 17th centuries. Its purpose was to demonstrate the productive power of humans as well as their enthusiasm.

Three aspects repeatedly appear in construction images. First, they symbolize the creativity and power of humans to overcome natural barriers. This symbolism is often found particularly in images of bridge and road construction. Second, the construction theme is personalized as the product of humans who act as independent construction engineers for their technical and social world. The erection of houses and great edifices often points to this symbolic meaning. Third, difficult construction work is often chosen to represent an idealized version of physical work, as in the example of the bronze worker on this page. In addition to these symbolic purposes, construction paintings are also of great interest to the technical history of the field as demonstrated by the paintings of the ECKHART G. GROHMANN COLLECTION and their descriptions on the following pages.

Boucher, Alfred [French, 1850-1934]: Worker With Shovel, bronze, 22 in., foundrymark "F. Barbedienne, Fondeu"

The intense effort of shoveling serves the artist well as a subject for neoclassical body study. This figure includes a Roman hairstyle and a complete muscular structure that is executed in exacting detail at the moment of the shoveler's greatest effort. Due to its precision, this statue could also be employed in labor or scientific and ergonomic studies. Beyond that, this statue serves as a symbol of work in general.

Studio of Hendrick van Cleve [Dutch, ca. 1525-ca. 1590]: The Tower of Babel, oil on panel, 19.5×27.5 in.

For more than a thousand years the myth of the construction of the *Tower of Babel* has been depicted in many paintings. This myth can be found illustrated in many cultures but the best known and clearest depiction is in the Old Testament in Genesis 11:1-9. The objective was to erect a tower all the way to the sky. In order to prevent this display of arrogance, God created many different languages so that the workers could not understand one another, and thus the project failed. The construction of the Tower of Babel is the third of three monumental works of mankind in Genesis. The first is farming and husbandry, developed after man's eviction from Paradise. Second was the construction of a large wooden ship, Noah's ark. Finally, the Tower of Babel, symbolizing man's increasing technical competence, and perhaps more importantly, the arrogance of mankind.

Since the middle ages, the pictorial presentations of this myth have been ambivalent. The tower inevitably remains unfinished, but the punishment of God is usually only weakly indicated, or left out entirely. The focus and emphasis is usually on a representation of human capability. Only rarely can you find such a drastic punishment of human arrogance, as in the etching by Heemskerck below.

The painting from the studio of Hendrik van Cleve comes from an era when hundreds of paintings depicting the Tower of Babel were created in the Netherlands. It shows the monumental, and as yet unfinished, project being admired by a group of the builder and his entourage. Numerous workers are busy with the preparation and transport of additional building materials.

Heemskerck, Marten van: The Tower of Babel, ca. 1580

Jacobsen, A.B.: Northern Industrial Landscape, oil on canvas, 15×23 in., 1934, signed

In clear, sharp lines reminiscent of an architectural rendering, Jacobsen paints an industrial brick-making facility in vivid colors of green, red, yellow and blue. The clay ingredients are carefully stored in yellow piles while the orderly stacks of burned red bricks are seen at the right. The scene is washed in sunlight. Conveyors and tall chimneys associated with the kilns characterize this painting, along with neat and orderly buildings. Neither people nor movement are visible, as in a still-life painting.

Hahn, Joseph [German, 1839-1906]: Brickworks
Reifenstuel at Bogenhausen, Germany, oil on canvas,
23.5×44 in., 1870, signed

The silhouette of the city of Munich is recognizable in the right background of this brick-making plant. As usual, the plant is located near a clay pit seen in the foreground, to minimize the transportation of the clay. First the raw bricks are dried, probably under the roofed structures to the left of the painting. The brickyard apparently has three kilns where the clay is baked at 800° C to 1000° C to form bricks. The artist not only portrays the work activity and the physical plant, but also creates an impressive landscape painting.

**Meunier, Constantin-Emile [Belgian, 1831-1905]:
Cabin of Brickworkers, oil on panel, 11×15.5 in.,
monogrammed "CM"**

This oil sketch by Meunier records the modest working conditions of brickworkers. Inside a makeshift accommodation, five laborers are clustered around a cooking facility with a kettle at the center of the painting. A fairly primitive brick stove is positioned along the right edge of the canvas. One board serves as a shelf. Upon this shelf there are several taps and other crockery items. One of the workmen is smoking a daypipe, as was customary among the Dutch.

Müller, Fritz [German, 1907-1999]: Autobahn Bridge Over Saale River Under Construction, Jena, Germany, oil on canvas, 31.5×27 in., signed

The construction of the Autobahn, or German national highway system, was driven by the *Third Reich* and based partly on earlier plans from the 1920s. It not only created employment for a large number of the unemployed and demonstrated the increasing power of the *Third Reich*, but also created a major military transportation asset. As with the other major projects of the Hitler regime, the workers were subjected to enormous propaganda. Many artists were commissioned to document the construction activities. The following pages offer a small but representative view of this group of construction paintings. Only a small portion of the many construction paintings by Erich Mercker gathered in the ECKHART G. GROHMANN COLLECTION are shown in this volume. A future special publication will deal with the entirety of Mercker's work. Bridges are the favorite subject of those who paint Autobahn construction scenes. In a special way, bridges embody the art of engineering, the productivity of construction, and the resulting accomplishment. In Müller's paintings, workers appear to play an insignificant role. Rather than a product of their labor, the bridge appears to be the work of the distant government in Berlin. The technical and historical aspects of these paintings are of great interest but, one should not underestimate their symbolic and political meaning.

**Mercker, Erich [German, 1891-1973]: Teufelstal
Autobahn Bridge Between Jena and Gera, Germany, oil
on cardboard, 16×20 in., signed**

Here Mercker intentionally presents a more impression-istic rather than a technical documentary view of a large Autobahn bridge construction. The power of the construction is emphasized by the view from below. The goldlike color of the bridge, together with the brilliant blue sky, results in an edification of the project normally seen only in religious structures. The "Bridges of the Führer" became the symbols of new Nazi rulers.

Mercker, Erich [German, 1891-1973]: Bridge
Construction at Havel River, Germany, oil on cardboard,
19×25 in., signed

The caisson construction method produces a foundation for a bridge pier in the river itself. Shown here are the required facilities at the job site. Two compressed air locks are seen above the scaffold. The workspace is between the driven interlocking piles of sheet steel and a horizontal reinforced concrete slab across the top of the sheet piles above the water line. Materials transported across the water are carried by a heavy rotating tower crane and smaller hoisting appliances to the individual spreading sites. Activities along the bank of the river related to the erection of the abutment and the subsequent roadway embankment are visible in the background.

Jacobsen, Fritz [German, 1867-1949]: Autobahn Bridge Construction, oil on panel, 31×42 in.

The structure shown in this picture spans a section of a valley at a considerable height. The four single concrete supports might be covered with natural stone. There are working scaffolds at the three supports; at one support there is also another scaffolding, most likely used for installing some final structural facing. In addition to that, a rotating tower crane set up at one pier serves as a vertical transportation facility for the required building materials.

Mercker, Erich [German, 1891-1973]: Construction of
Autobahn Bridge Over Werra River, Germany, oil on
canvas, 31.5×23.5 in., signed

This picture displays the assembly of the solid-walled rectangular box unit belonging to a steel parallel main girder of the Autobahn Bridge across the Werra River. An assembly operation, employing the method of cantilever construction, has been made possible by a temporary guy wire structure set above one of the towers designed to accept the already long cantilevered section of the bridge. At the end of the cantilevered boom there is a traveling derrick crane used for the piece-by-piece joining of the individual girder elements.

Dieninghoff, Wilhelm [German, 1903-1984]: Autobahn
Construction, Munich-Salzburg 1936, oil on panel,
32×42 in., ca. 1936, signed

This section of the Munich-Salzburg Autobahn crosses a valley in the Chiemsee-Traunstein area. The steel super-structure is borne at its points of support by two concrete piers, which are linked to one another by means of a tie beam to become a frame. The construction workers in the foreground are busy reconfiguring the earth to widen the access road to produce a highway junction. Workers move soil piles manually with the help of the picks and shovels as the roadway is leveled in preparation for additional work.

Mercker, Erich [German, 1891-1973]: Autobahn in Palatine, Germany, oil on cardboard, 16×20.5 in., signed

With simple but effective brush strokes and color application, Mercker produces a typical impression of the German Autobahn of his time. The double lane expressway of cast concrete plates causes rumbling noises and vibrations similar to that experienced while riding the contemporary railroad.

Mercker, Erich [German, 1891-1973]: Construction of Rohrbach Bridge Near Stuttgart, Germany, oil on academy board, 15×19 in., signed

The Rohrbach Bridge near Stuttgart, Germany, completed in 1936, crosses the Rohrbach Valley as a parallel structure of reinforced concrete arches. Both pictures show the erection of the twin concrete arch ribs. Surveying and form building are apparently underway in the foreground of the upper picture. In the lower picture, the rear arch shown in the foreground has not yet been stripped of its wooden form. The concrete work is produced with great mechanical effort and skill and enables one to draw some conclusions concerning the enormous costs of the construction. The roadway plate does not rest directly on the arches, but rather on eight symmetrically arranged columns per arch. In this way, the finished roadway appears to be hovering above the line of arches.

Mercker, Erich [German, 1891-1973]: Bridge Construction With Arcs, oil on canvas, 23.5×31.5 in., signed

**Mercker, Erich [German, 1891-1973]: Construction
of Bridge Over Rhine at Frankenthal-Mannheim,
Germany, oil on cardboard, 14×19 in., signed**

Mercker portrays the assembly of a beam bridge for the German Autobahn crossing the Rhine River. The superstructure of box beam construction has been largely completed. The final section has been assembled from prefabricated pieces and lies on its assembly scaffold on the riverbank. A floating crane will hoist it to its exact river location below the assembly. The derrick cranes on the cantilevered ends of the bridge assembly will raise the part to its ultimate position where it will be fixed in place. The picture displays the preparations being taken in anticipation of the installation of this box unit, here seen with a red lead coating for protection against corrosion. Apparently, a portion of the superstructure has already received such a coating.

Mercker, Erich [German, 1891-1973]: Rhine Bridge Construction, Cologne, Germany, oil and pastel on canvas, 31×39 in., ca. 1940, signed

Mercker, Erich [German, 1891-1973]: Bridge Construction, Cologne-Mülheim, Germany, oil on cardboard, 15×20 in., signed

Mercker, Erich [German, 1891-1973]: Bridge Construction, Cologne-Mülheim, Germany, oil on cardboard, 15×19 in., signed

The pictures on these two pages record various construction stages of the suspension bridge across the Rhine River at Cologne. Both end abutments, anchoring blocks, and foundation piers of the pylons have already been completed. Both steel frame-shaped pylons have been set up by means of portal cranes, and the cables they support are already spanning the river. The rectangular reinforcement girder sections of the bridge, probably prefabricated in workshops, are being lifted onto the assembly scaffold with the help of a floating crane. There the girders are con-

Mercker, Erich [German, 1891-1973]: Construction of
Rhine Bridge at Night, oil on canvas, 23×31 in., signed

nected to the section already in place, as displayed in the first three pictures. The picture above shows the assembly of the reinforcement girders within the electric power section at an advanced construction state where the suspension cables have already been connected. The nighttime assembly operation by means of two floating cranes suggests that the joining of the individual box units, including their mounting to the suspension cables, must have been carried out while all water traffic was halted.

Aranha, Simão [Portuguese, 1908-2000]: Bridge Over Tagus River (Golden Gate Bridge) of Lisbon Under Construction, oil on panel, 24×35 in., 1965, signed

This last bridge construction painting shows the Lisbon Bridge over the Tagus River, very similar to the San Francisco *Golden Gate Bridge*. The bridge was built by the *United States Steel Company* from 1962 to 1966. More than a thousand meters in length, it was the largest bridge outside the United States. Aranha painted it in 1965 while it was under construction. By the right end of the bridge stands the statue "Christo-Rei," similar to that in Rio de Janeiro. The statue was built to thank God for keeping Portugal out of World War II.

Lehmann, Ludwig Wilhelm [1861-1932]: Wagithal
Dam Near Zurich, Switzerland, oil on plaque, 31×21 in.,
signed

A tunnel exit of the water dam under construction can be seen in the foreground. Most likely it is a concrete gravity dam, since no reinforcement bars are visible. There is a concrete mixing plant located at the top of the mountain. Several cable car systems are in operation to deliver construction materials. At the center, a cable car system delivers concrete to the site. The supply of materials is apparently arranged via an inclined hoist in the right background. In addition, two pipelines for conveying concrete are suspended from cables on the right.

Mercker, Erich [German, 1891-1973]: Construction of
Hydro Power Plant, Füssen-Rosshaupten, Germany, oil
on cardboard, 19×19 in., signed

**Mercker, Erich [German, 1891-1973]: Construction
of Isar Hydro Works, Pfronbach, Germany, oil on
cardboard, 14×19 in., signed**

Controlling and utilizing the power of water has not only
a practical, but also a highly symbolic, meaning in history,
rather analogous to historical treatment of fire. Both of
these paintings by Mercker illustrate the geological and
technical challenges of building waterpowered generating
plants. The choice of this subject and Mercker's treatment
of it also demonstrates the powerful effect of water control on humans in modern society. Even in ancient times
the ability to control water was a result and symbol of
political power. Just consider the irrigation-based cultures
on the Euphrates and Tigris Rivers in Mesopotamia.

This picture establishes workers' lodging during the building period at a large construction site by using prefabricated components and employing a small rotating tower crane. In the background a steam-operated field railroad engine pulls several cargo trucks. Excavation activities for a foundation are being performed in the foreground.

Mercker, Erich [German, 1891-1973]: Construction of Residential Buildings Near Oberammergau, Germany, oil on canvas on board, 13.5×19.5 in., signed

This painting depicts preparation of concrete for the erection of an additional barracks building. The carpenters are completing the scaffolding for the partition walls. The conveyance of the building materials is arranged in individual skips. The change in directions at the intersectional points is implemented via manually-operated turntables.

Mercker, Erich [German, 1891-1973]: Construction Site, Ludwigsplatz, Munich, Germany, oil on canvas, 16×19 in., signed

Mercker, Erich [German, 1891-1973]: Construction of the U-Boat Lock at La Rochelle, France, oil on cardboard, 18×27 in., 1943, signed

During World War II, the Germans constructed military facilities in France. Behind a cofferdam consisting of two vertical sheet piles, concrete is poured for a new dry dock used in the construction of submarines. The scene is inside a harbor edged with jetties, one of which is joined to the mainland by means of a steel truss bridge.

Mercker, Erich [German, 1891-1973]: Congress Hall in Nuremberg Under Construction, Germany, oil on academy board, 15×19 in., signed

This painting portrays the construction of the reviewing grandstand for the *Zeppelin Airfield,* a portion of the *Nazi Party Convention Center* in Nuremberg. Built of Jurassic limestone, it was almost a quarter mile long, 80 feet tall, and seated an audience of 64,000.

Mercker, Erich [German, 1891-1973]: Rebricking the
Blast Furnace at Linz, Austria, oil on canvas, 23×31 in.,
signed.

The inside lining of a blast furnace is eventually eaten
away by the high-temperature process taking place within. To avoid a disastrous break in the wall, a blast furnace
occasionally must be taken out of service and rebricked.
Because of lost production, this is a time of intense effort.
The new bricks for relining are visible in the foreground.

A crane to move the construction material stands to the
right. Bracing bars are welded to the outer body of the
blast furnace for increased strength. Two recuperators are
seen to the left of each blast furnace. The tip of a second
crane extends from behind the second blast furnace.

Mercker, Erich [German, 1891-1973]: Rep. R. Allianz,
Steel Mill, oil on cardboard, 15×19 in., signed

An expansion of a boiler house at the *Allianz Power Plant* is seen at the center of the painting. Building cranes and steelworkers are busy. The power plant is still operational, as indicated by the fumes leaving the central chimney and by the condensing steam released by the powerhouse to the right. A coal pile served by an overhead traveling loading bridge is shown in front of the power plant. The grain field in the foreground is in juxtaposition to industry, a popular theme at the time.

Sandrock, Leonhard [German, 1867-1945]:
Construction Work on the Crane of a Converter, oil on
canvas, 12.6×10.2 in., signed

The top of a blast furnace is under reconstruction or repair. Much of the activity is on the platform of the furnace top bell in the lower part of the painting. To the left is the hemispherical dome of a recuperator, while mist from a neighboring active blast furnace is to the right. The inclined conveyor delivers ore, coke, lime and other ingredients to charge the blast furnace. The two vertical beams are involved in the bleeding of gases during part of the process.

**Multrus, Josef: Workers Moving Heavy Building Block,
oil on cardboard, 18×23 in., ca. 1930, signed**

Three workers heave a heavy building stone onto a conveyer system. From there, the stone travels in a small rail car to the building site for installation. This appears to be a large construction project. The fourth worker stands on another rail car riding on a second track. Next to him sits an even larger stone ready to be transported.

Frenes, Rud. Hir. [1846-1916]: Five People at House Construction, oil on panel, 11×16 in., ca. 1900, signed

Bricklayers are shown at work. The bricks are not being positioned as normal along a marked line; instead some vertical laths have been set up to guide the process. The brickwork is not laid in a flush manner, perhaps because the bricklayers may be using old bricks. Both the women in the background are watching the workers' efforts and may be serving as helpers.

Mercker, Erich [German, 1891-1973]: Brick Layers, oil on cardboard, 19.5×19.5 in., ca. 1935, signed

Several bricklayers and laborers are working together in a very confined space, possibly inferring a short construction schedule. There seems to be no employment of machinery to assist the workers as they build pillars. The transportation of bricks and mortar is totally manual.

Vladimirov, Ivan [Russian, 1869-1947]: Clearing Mountain Road of a Boulder, oil on canvas, 17.5×25 in., signed

Construction workers are moving irregular stones off a future road surface by employing large levers. Behind this central scene, surveyors are at work with helpers holding the staff for the leveling operations to the upper right of the painting. Two steam-powered excavators are waiting for their assignments.

Markó, Lajos [Hungarian, *1882]: Tunnel Construction, oil on paper, 20×24 in., signed

Six tunnel workers are attempting to move an immobilized cart. A factory looms in the background. This painting employs a common allegory of hard labor, symbolized by the extremely demanding work of tunnel construction.

Pushing, pulling and carrying of heavy loads generally symbolize the burdens of human beings in the iconography of the working picture.

Lommen, Wilhelm [German, 1839-1895]: Stone
Transport With Horseteam, oil on canvas, 24.5×37 in.,
1878, signed

This horse-drawn wagon transports stones through a wide valley apparently undergoing industrial development. The wagon is probably loaded with cobblestones, which will be used to pave more roads to serve the expanding industrial base. This painting depicts the years of the greatest German industrial development of the 19th century, and demonstrates the interdependence of the various industrial sectors of the economy.

Brandenberg, Wilhelm [German, *1889]: Steamroller at Road Construction, oil on canvas, 32×40 in., 1937, signed

A village path is being widened to a two-lane road. The steamroller compresses the new crushed rock. The old fences still lining the road can be seen along the left edge of the painting. Behind the house is a railroad rack with a stationary cargo car. To the right are the timber poles to supply electricity and telephone service, running parallel to the railroad track.

Mercker, Erich [German, 1891-1973]: Civil
Engineering, Türkenstraße, Munich, oil on cardboard,
18×18 in., ca. 1935, signed

The scene looks across an open construction pit to the other side. An access ladder to the pit is in the foreground. The activities concern the construction of a major piece of the sewerage system in the *Türkenstraße,* or *Turk Street,* in Munich. The presence of the cut steel beams suggest that they will be driven into the ground as piles to reinforce the edge of the construction pit. Horse-drawn carts convey the building materials. A steam-powered cable winch excavator is operating in the background. A limousine is parked on the left, but the gentleman wearing a hat is not the construction company owner. If he were, he would attract a great deal more attention.

Schulze-Görlitz, Johvi: "Trümmerfrauen"(Rubble Women) Reclaiming Bricks After World War II, oil on canvas, 36×31 in., 1951, signed

Following World War II, many German cities lay in ruins. Millions of German men had died in the war or remained in prisoner-of-war confinements. Rebuilding required everyone's help. Women were especially needed to assist in the removal of debris to make rebuilding possible. They made history as "Trümmerfrauen," or "rubble women." Here the women are shown gathering and cleaning bricks from bombed-out buildings, for reuse in new construction.

Holan, Karel: Corner House Under Construction, oil on cardboard, 17.7×24.5 in., signed

A corner building is under construction on a cold winter day. Additional stores will be added, as can be seen from the high scaffolding. The artist does not deal with technical detail nor with the working process. Rather, he presents the productive building activity of a commune created for its members.

Howald, Lothar [German, *1915]: Scaffolded
Brandenburg Gate, Berlin, Germany, oil on canvas,
19×23 in., 1951, signed

The *Brandenburg Gate*, a German icon built in 1791, was damaged in the battle of Berlin during World War II. In this postwar painting, a Soviet-Russian flag is flying on top of the *Brandenburg Gate*, which originally separated the center of town from the suburbs. It was regarded as a symbol both of the division and unity of Germany until reunification in 1989. The former sentry shed can be identified to the right side of the scaffolding. The rebuilding process moves forward with masons working on the blocks of stone. Two derrick cranes are available to lift the heavy pieces of stone.

H.B., monogrammed: Hard Construction Work, Triptychon,
oil on canvas, 34.5×34.5 in., 34.5×45.5 in., 34.5×34.5 in.

The triptychon format of these paintings originated in religious altar art. When employed in a secular manner, as in this case, it is intended to celebrate a very important special occasion. This triptychon probably was created shortly after World War II. At the left is the mining of clay material for building tile, while the right panel shows the extrusion of tiles with emphasis on the women workers. The central panel shows four bricklayers lining a tall

building with clay building blocks. The heavy fired blocks are lined up with wooden wedges, in a manner similar to that of natural stone work, and are fixed to the masonry by mortar. Several completed buildings are in the background, which may be new buildings lining *Stalin Avenue* in East Berlin.

Konecny, Josef [*1909]: Mortar Mixing for Power Plant Construction in South Moravia, Czechoslovakia, oil on canvas, 24.5×20.5 in., 1952, signed

This painting illustrates a small portion of a power plant construction site. One worker mixes mortar while another pushes a lift bucket full of mortar and other building materials to other workstations. The building is constructed of steel and concrete. The site is in Moravia, an area of Czechoslovakia at the time of the painting, and today part of the Czech Republic. This picture is intended to proclaim the progress of the socialistic state.

Hartig, Fred [1901-1973]: Construction Worker With Wheelbarrow, oil on canvas, 51×40 in., monogrammed "F.H."

A construction worker pushes a wooden wheelbarrow up a timber incline over a base that appears to be excavated earth and construction scraps. To the right, a bricklayer works on a scaffold. Houses and storefronts are visible in the background.

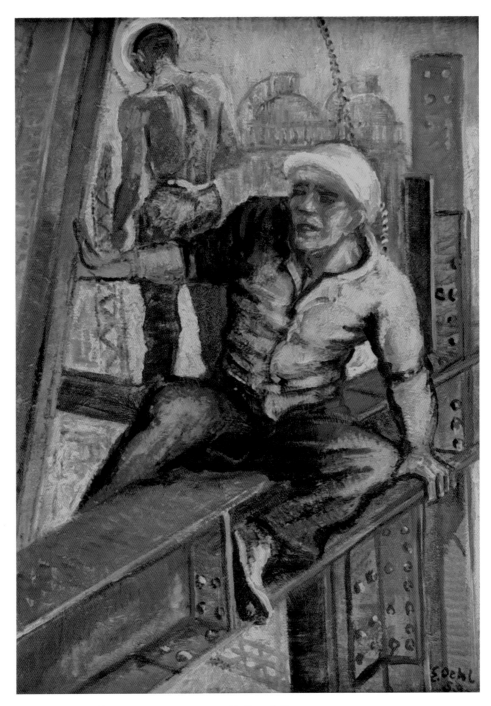

Oehl, Erwin [German, 1907-1988]: Steel Construction Worker, oil on canvas, 20.5×15.4 in., 1952, signed

Oehl was a social critic and artist who was an active opponent of the German occupation of France in World War II. This painting likely bids homage to the highly regarded French artist Theophile Steinlen, whose famous 1908 painting *The Steel Workers* served as an allegory for his wish for a victory of the working class. Oehl's confidence appears to have begun to wane. His sympathy is still with the worker, but the painting is missing the triumphant pose of Steinlen's work.

Pieper, Josef [German, 1907-1977]: Big Crane, oil on
canvas, 39×47.5 in., signed

A derrick is mounted on a floating pontoon. The two main beams of the derrick are connected. The lifting pulley systems are coupled together by a transverse connection. The pulleys each have a six-fold mechanical advantage. Several additional hooks and pulleys enable control of the load. Construction workers are on the dock; one works with an air hammer, apparently performing ship repair work. In the foreground lies a sheet metal portion of a ship's hull.

**Müller, Fritz [German, 1907-1999]: On the Ground of
the Dam at Hohenwarte, oil on cardboard, 28×30 in.,
1958, signed**

The large dam at Hohenwarte holds back the waters of the
Saale River in Thuringia. The artist illustrates the excavation and earth moving. On the left stands the construction
manager with blueprints. A large shovel on chain treads is
set to work. The round, green device in the left foreground
is a pump to drive the water from the work site.

Piltz, Otto [German, 1846-1910]: Lunch Break in Tunnel, oil on panel, 22×18 in., 1878, signed

A cavern provides a lunchroom for a group of workers. Women and men eat meals they have brought from home. The supervisor sits in the background, somewhat separate from the group. The scene could represent a group of day workers building a mountain road. The workers' tasks are not clear since no tools are shown in the picture. The aprons worn by the men may indicate they are masons, while the women are probably assisting with the supply of building materials.

5. Timber

Lumber is one of the oldest natural resources used by humans. Wood remains a vital raw material today for the construction of houses, furniture and tools. After transformation into charcoal, wood serves as a fuel for cooking, heating dwellings, and for the manufacture of paper and many other products. For many years charcoal was used to fuel blast furnaces. In the course of history, humans have consumed large portions of the world's forest. After a catastrophic shortage of lumber in Europe in the 18th century caused by extensive destruction of natural forests, a systematic forestry management program was developed. For many people, forests and wood products represent an emotional connection with nature, a feeling also evident in art. Paintings of lumberjacks, lumber carts, carpenters and barrel makers, or coopers, are mostly calm and friendly. They present a somewhat romantic atmosphere in contrast to the clearly hectic paintings of steel mills and ironworkers. The ECKHART G. GROHMANN COLLECTION contains a small but very fine component of artworks from this area.

Anonymous [Japanese]: Japanese Sawer, ivory and cast iron, 7.5×11 in., 19th c.

This beautiful sculpture carved from ivory depicts a Japanese woodcutter. He uses a wide iron saw to produce one board after another from a large tree trunk – perhaps teakwood. Using a wide saw blade makes it is easier to manage a straight cut, provided the initial cut into the wood is straight. This work requires great precision and care and represents a very slow process. The tedious work almost gives the impression of an Asian meditation exercise.

Jacques, Napoléon [French, 1804-1876]: Lumberman, bronze, 16.75 in., 1852, signed "N. Jacques St. Petersbourg. 1852"

This bronze statue depicts a Russian woodworker in the middle of the 19th century. The artist is from St. Petersburg and depicts the woodworker dressed in a typical Russian coat and belt, long pants with boots, and a sweatband over his head. The woodworker employs a broad ax to cut a wide kerf, apparently intending to shorten a rectangular wood block. He is prepared for the day with a pitcher next to his left leg, and a loose sack tied by two strings that holds his next meal. The iron stake on the ground alludes to the next step of installing the railroad tie.

Unknown [American]: Woodcutters at Work, oil on canvas, 11.5×15.5 in., signed

The subject, structure and colors of this painting are reminiscent of English artist John Constable. On a beautiful fall day, lumberjacks are working at the forest edge with a view into an expansive valley. Two horses pull tree trunks out of the forest to be sawed by the two workers in the foreground using a common large saw. At the center, an oxcart is waiting to be loaded. A woman prepares a fortifying meal at the fire next to a small shelter.

Pocci, Xaveria Gräfin von [German, 1778-1849]: Saw Mill in the Morning, oil on canvas, 13×17 in., 1845, monogrammed "P"

The sawmill is powered by an overshot water wheel, currently not in operation. The incomplete slide for the sawmill operation can be identified lying next to the building. This slide drives the saw and is operated by means of linkage bars that run across the workshop. A laborer is busily at work on the sawmill platform, while a child sits on the corner of the platform enjoying the sunshine. The attic, not needed for any sawmill activities, is utilized as a hay barn. The finished timber boards are taken out of the mill and piled in an interesting pattern, exposing them to the air for drying. The first light of day is filling the romantically painted valley.

Lommen, Wilhelm [German, 1839-1895]: Pulling Log With Horseteam, oil on canvas, 19×25 in., signed

A three-horse team draws a heavy tree trunk from the forest to the sawmill on a single axle cart. Due to the extremely heavy load, a worker helps to push the cart uphill. The draw horses clearly feel the strain, caused primarily by the heavy log dragging on the dirt road. Employing a two-axle cart would help alleviate the load. The artist's choice for the horses' colors, including black, white and reddish-brown, may be a symbolic representation of the national colors of the German empire.

**Wouters, Bouter Cornelius [1888-1966]: The Log Cart,
oil on canvas, 23×31 in.**

The lumberworker makes his last adjustments in loading a large tree trunk onto a special transport cart. The tree trunk still drags on the ground but does not need to be raised as high, because the log is suspended below the axle. The huge wheels help to facilitate the transport by making bumps and ruts less significant. The two horses standing at rest wear blinders, indicating that the route may involve some busy streets. The tree was cut in late fall when the tree sap is at a minimum.

This painting by Carl Wilhelm Kolbe the Younger offers a view into the 16th century. The year 1568 appears on the wooden plane tool standing in the lower right corner of the picture. In that year the famous *Book on Trades* by Jost Amman was published. Therefore, this painting may be interpreted as a romantic tribute to the ancient trade of the cooper, or barrel maker. The center of the painting illustrates the finishing of an especially large wine cask. Three journeymen are busily hammering accurately sized rings onto the barrel. To the left, in a red shirt and leather apron, stands the red-cheeked master, who critically observes the finishing of the cask with his customers. To the left is another person, perhaps an apprentice. What appears to be the master's wife and children are in the foreground, painted as cupids. Another assistant on the right carries a planing tool and gives the impression he is waiting for the ring the child is playing with. The scene shows an open workshop framed by wine stalks. This layout, with the group of figures to the right and the angel-like children, resembles the composition and atmosphere of the popular presentations of the Holy Family at that time. The person to the right of the wife is positioned like the figure of Joseph and carries a carpenter's tool. The grape arbor corresponds to the partially open roof of the stable at Bethlehem. The distant view is of a south German landscape and the silhouette of a medieval town.

This painting has a special history. It inspired the German romantic writer E.T.A. Hoffmann to write the novel *Master Martin, the Cooper and His Journeyman*. Hoffmann had borrowed this painting from Kolbe and commissioned a modified etching of the painting seen at right for the first edition of his novel. In historical literature this painting is still listed as missing to this day. Now, as a part of the ECKHART G. GROHMANN COLLECTION at the *Milwaukee School of Engineering*, it can be studied and admired by Hoffmann researchers and admirers.

Hoffmann's novel deals with the selection of the best husband for the beautiful daughter of the master cooper Martin. Only a cooper may marry his daughter, Rosa, and only one who is able to build a perfect, especially large, cask. Three journeymen apply and it slowly becomes evident that none of them are trained coopers. After all sorts of confusion, a happy ending ensues when a goldsmith eventually marries the daughter. The second suitor, a painter, composes a painting for the wedding portraying the master with his three journeymen working on a large cask, while Rosa is just entering the area. Kolbe then painted an additional painting matching that description. The etching by Schmidt shows Rosa, but only two journeymen. Hoffmann's novel is set in Nuremberg at the time of Hans Sachs, who composed the verses

Etching by H. Schmidt for E.T.A. Hoffmann's novel *Meister Martin, der Küfner und seine Gesellen*, 1818, Staatsbibliothek Bamberg

Kolbe, Carl Wilhelm, the Younger [German, 1781-1853]: Cooper Shop, Old German in 1568, oil on panel, 16.5×21.5 in., ca. 1816, signed

for Amman's *Book of Trades*. Like Kolbe's painting, the novel praises the traditional trades that slowly vanished during the 19th century. Hoffmann also describes a tradition of the trades in *The Master Sing-* *ing*. In turn, this is thought to have inspired Richard Wagner to compose his famous opera *The Master Singers*. So the trail leads from this painting by Kolbe to that famous and popular Wagnerian opera.

Bill, Lina [French, 1855-1936]: Cooper, oil on canvas,
28×40 in., ca. 1920, signed

This cooper is fitting an iron band to the barrel to determine the correct length for joining the hoop around the barrel. The barrel is not exactly a masterpiece, since the wooden staves are of irregular construction and made out of inferior lumber. It does not appear destined for the aging of precious wine. The bunghole is already bored. On the wood block to the left sits a broad ax used to produce a smooth surface on the wood. On top of the barrel is a special tool, probably used to additionally smooth the wooden surfaces.

Mieth, Hugo [Bohemian, *1865]: Large Barrelmaking Shop, oil on canvas, 40×38 in., signed

A well-lit cooper's workshop is illustrated. The artist focuses primarily on the interaction of light, color and space to create atmosphere in the workshop. The production process itself is only a secondary issue, shown on the left. The absent worker is apparently in the process of trimming the upper edge of a new barrel. In contrast to the cooper in Lina Bill's painting, common convex barrels are not made here. Rather, a conical-shaped design is produced. A finished barrel sits next to the staircase.

Smith, Arthur Reginald [English, 1871-1934]: The Wheelwright, watercolor, 11×15.5 in., 1905, signed

This impressionistic watercolor shows the interior of an English wheelwright's forge. At the center, the master works on a highlighted carriage wheel, which rests on a three-legged wooden stand. The rough construction of the wheel rim is complete and the hub and spokes are already mounted. The wheelwright stands at his workbench by the window, deeply absorbed in his work. The floor is covered by wood shavings – a picturesque touch to an extraordinarily sensitive painting honoring a vanished trade.

**Olivié-Bon, Léon [French, 1863-1901]: The Apprentice,
oil on canvas, 53×32 in., 1889, signed**

This painting originated during the French realism period when the so-called "common folk" became respectable subjects, worthy of painting. It is notable that a lowly woodworking apprentice is portrayed here resting and not working. The artist is primarily depicting an uncomplicated lifestyle. The lumber storage bay of a substantial joiner's workshop is illustrated. The woodworker toils at a large joiner's bench with three wood planes. Another bench stands to the left, and several hand saws hang from a support.

Dexter, Walter [British, *1876]: The Carpenter's Workshop, oil on canvas, 30×25 in., 1904, signed

Walter Dexter evokes an emotional atmosphere with his painting of a carpenter in his workshop. Judging from the tools around him, this is a capable furniture maker. The craftsman forms a piece of wood with a mallet and chisel. In front of him on his workbench lies a large hand plane to provide a smooth finish to large wooden boards. A pot of glue heats up over a flame at the lower left. The bottles probably contain stain to color the wood. The carpenter relies on daylight. The kerosene lamp hanging from the ceiling would provide insufficient light to work at night.

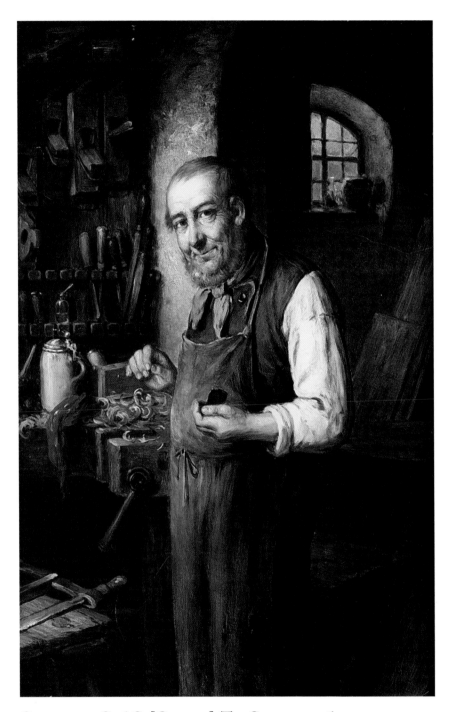

Ostersetzer, Carl C. [German]: The Carpenter, oil on panel, 18.5×12 in., 1906, signed

The contented carpenter takes a break from his work to pose for a portrait. With a pipe in his left hand and a beer stein on his workbench, he faces the observer. Wood chips and a red handkerchief are picturesquely displayed on his workbench. The scene is a typical genre painting of its time. To the extent it portrayed a trade or profession the objective was always to depict the typical work environment. To a greater degree than is experienced today, a lifelong occupation at this time formed the persona of a man.

**Henley, Lionel Charles [British, 1843-1893]: Ship
Carpenter at His Hobby, oil on canvas, 23.5×16 in., signed**

Here is another genre painting. The ship carpenter is so attached to his profession that even after retirement he feels the attraction to configure wooden ships – just much smaller than before. He adjusts the mast of an almost completed sailing ship model. He has acquired various tools for his hobby. In the foreground he has a collection of various ropes. To the left stands a wine pitcher for refreshment. He resides in what is probably a small dwelling with a view of the beach and ocean, which are important to him.

6. Leather and Textiles

The production of textiles and leather goods is very fundamental to satisfying basic human needs. Since antiquity, the production of textiles has been a recurring theme in art. This is partly based on myths and legends, especially those involving spinning and weaving. It is also due to the fact that textile production has been associated with the home and in-home activity since the Middle Ages. In preindustrial society, textile work belonged in the women's domain. Even in the industrial age, embroidery, sewing and knitting were expressions of home-based women. Spinning and weaving, however, moved out of the home and were among the earliest activities to be industrialized. The great demand for clothing, particularly for the wealthy and the military, offered the promise of good profitability.

Brekelenkam, Quiringh Gerritsz van [Dutch, after 1622-1668]: A Cobbler, oil on panel, 22×32 in., 1650-60, monogrammed "Q VB"

This painting is from the Golden Age of Dutch painting. Brekelenkam is one of the most important artists to depict common people in their living and working environments. The cobbler was the symbol of the poorest of tradeworkers. In this picture, a female customer is waiting for a shoe repair that a cobbler does in his modest workshop. To gain better daylight he works on an elevated platform. His wife pours a drink from a barrel, which is being siphoned into a beautiful pitcher in the foreground.

Schneider, B. [†1900]: Munich Shoemaker, oil on cardboard, 23×20 in., signed

Shoemakers are usually shown as individualists living under poor conditions. They never held a significant role in the hierarchy of the trade guilds. The cobblers in these two paintings are intent on their work. The cobbler above nails a new sole onto a shoe while it is drawn over a shoemaker's anvil. The second shoe of the pair sits in the foreground. At

Skorikow, Jurii [Russian, *1824]: Shoemaker, oil on canvas, 25×19 in., signed

the left you see a new shoe drawn over a wooden shoehorn to yield the correct size and shape. Another tool is within reach. The Russian shoemaker in Skorikov's painting seems to be putting the finishing touches to a new black leather shoe. A hearty drink is ready for refreshment. The workshop seems to be in very poor condition.

Mende, Carl Adolf [German, 1807-1857]: Shoemaker's Workshop, oil on canvas, 18×21.5 in., 1834, signed

The cobbler's platform is elevated in front of the window in order to have the best light conditions. The apprentices are industriously involved in their work. The young boy by the window is occupying an unusual seating arrangement. With his one-legged stool he can easily find another place to work anywhere inside the room, but he chooses the elevated platform. The second apprentice, seated on a three-legged stool, seems to be disturbing his master by asking him a question while the latter is immersed in reading the *Bayrischer Landbote*, a local newspaper. The central roof beam supports two glass objects containing substances to attract or repel insects, a predecessor of "fly paper."

Crespi, Giuseppe Maria [Italian, 1665-1747, attributed]:
Peasants Making Silk; Carrying and Spreading Cocoons,
oil on canvas, 23×29 in.

Silk has been cultivated in China since antiquity. During the first centuries after the birth of Christ, silk in Greece was valued the same as gold by weight. In the sixth century the Roman Empire planted mulberry bushes for the purpose of raising silkworms. During the 17th and 18th centuries, silkworms were raised in many European countries. Crespi's painting shows a large group of women spreading silkworm cocoons for sorting and drying under the Italian sun. The window at the upper left shows a gentle lady spinning silk. This is probably a larger-scale silk processor.

Hoelscher, Richard [German, 1867-1943]: Boy
Spinning Yarn, oil on canvas, 24.5×17.5 in., 1898, signed

With his left hand the boy is guiding the thread onto the spool. His right hand is moving a large wheel with a crank handle. The spool is operated via a rope. To the right corner of the painting is a reel coiling device, displaying the process in which the yarn leaves a dyeing shop. Before the yarn can be sold it has to be coiled onto spools. On top of the rack along the wall are bags containing dyed yarn. Above it are two birdcages with birds inside that serve as a distraction from the monotonous work.

**Eichstaedt, Rudolf [German, 1857-1924]: Dutch
Spooling Woman, oil on panel, 37.5×31 in., 1890, signed**

Young Dutch women working at textile activities were an extraordinarily attractive theme for many painters. Attractiveness, industriousness, color and light were composed into a plain genre painting. This young woman transfers the thread with the help of a simple wooden spinning wheel onto a wooden spool. This must be done carefully, layer by layer, so the thread can flow freely without any problems when used at the next workstation. In the foreground are sacks of raw wool, which the woman still must spin.

Towards the end of the 19ᵗʰ century, industrial painting was already established and Menzel's *Iron Rolling Mill* was a celebrated example. However, socially realistic paintings of common working folks still created scandals and were received with disapproval.

Max Liebermann, later to become one of the most famous German painters, experienced the same response. This was particularly true of depictions of working women that did not fit the popular ideal of beauty. These paintings were banned from the prevailing academic art. Until about 1900 Liebermann devoted his efforts to the realistic, and yet socially and politically benign, depiction of work as a theme. He dealt exclusively with nonindustrial subjects. In his work *Flax Barn in Laren*, he depicted preindustrial spinning, although this obsolete production process was already adapting to industrial manufacturing.

A large number of women and children spin the prepared flax to raw yarn. This is accomplished by a process that combines methods from the classical working at home and a true factory. Twelve women and girls twist the flax into thread and onto spools, employing spool machines at the left below the windows, that are powered by children. Two female spinners work with each spinning machine. These machines are probably the so-called Mule-Jenny-spinning machines developed in England perhaps 10 years before this painting. The spinning machine was developed from two previous machines and was sometimes driven by other sources, such as water or steam power. But, when cheap labor was available, as was the case with women and children in Holland, they were employed. At the left background a

Liebermann, Max: Flax Barn in Laren, oil on canvas, 1887, Staatliche Museen zu Berlin – Preußischer Kulturbesitz, Nationalgalerie

Liebermann, Max [German, 1847-1935]: Study for *Flax Barn in Laren,* oil on board laid down on panel, 20.5×31 in., 1886, signed

young woman apparently repairs a machine, while at her right more flax is introduced. Everyone is working intently, concentrating to avoid any break in the thread. Conversation, a characteristic of work in the home environment as well as in the earlier groups of spinners, is not possible here.

The most complete study for this famous painting by Liebermann is in the ECKHART G. GROHMANN COLLECTION. The scene has been extensively discussed and analyzed in literature, sometimes raising controversy. The basic question is whether Liebermann created this painting with a critical intent, or to portray the positive values of work in this more structured environment. Whatever the answer, this painting is not only an outstanding work of art, but also important documentation of a historic work process.

**Kiekebusch, Albert Gustav Adolf [German, *1861]:
Linen Weaver at Her Loom, oil on canvas, 20×18.5 in.,
1888, signed**

This worker weaves yarn produced from the flax into linen cloth. Before industrialization of the weaving process, weaving was done at home for one's own use, and sometimes for others, on looms like the one in this painting.

The weaving process combines the planes of yarn running in the direction of the weaver with a single piece of yarn the shuttle carries back and forth between these planes and perpendicular to the many strands of yarn.

**Henckel, Karl [German, *1881]: Old Woman Working
Loom, oil on canvas, 38×35.5 in., signed**

With sunlight streaming past a flower on the windowsill, an experienced female weaver pursues her work. On a heavy loom she produces linen for sale to supplement the family's modest income. By this time, this handmade process was completely replaced by the much more efficient machine weaving mills. Even so, at the time this picture was probably painted in the 1930s this type of textile production still existed in remote rural areas.

Stock, Carl [German, 1876-1945]: Tanner, bronze, 15.5 in., 1924, signed

The production of leather from animal hides is a process of multiple steps. Tanning starts only after a complete cleansing of the skin of all hair and fat. During tanning any residual animal protein turns into crystals. With a set of long tongs the tanner submerges the skin in an acid bath. This is a very unpleasant job.

Meyer-Pyritz [German, 1870-1942]: Fabric Dyer, bronze, 16.5 in., signed

The dyeworker on the right inspects the color and uniformity of material following the coloring process. His left hand employs a stick to avoid touching the cloth, and to prevent the cloth from touching the floor.

7. FARMING

The portrayal of farm work permeates the cultural history of human society over thousands of years. Farming the soil, growing and utilizing plants and animals, and the additional processing of plant and animal products, represent the basis of all human existence. Farming always results in an immediate confrontation with nature. As long as humans accepted that gods controlled and dominated nature, the resulting myths, rites and legends grew around farm activities, particularly with regards to plowing, sewing, harvesting and spinning.

In the past, life on the farm was valued very differently. On the one hand, it was the most primitive form of life and work. On the other hand, since the time of ancient Rome, farm life was praised and romanticized, especially by the bourgeois, as a world of happiness and the only natural lifestyle. We also find these two faces of farming in the visual arts at the beginning of the 20th century.

The relatively small amount of farm-related art in the ECKHART G. GROHMANN COLLECTION dates mostly from the end of the 19th century. In that period, social-realistic portrayals are typical, along with romantic presentations.

Remington, Frederic [American, 1861-1909]: The Bronco Buster, bronze, 23×20 in., signed, foundrymark "Roman Bronze"

This bronco buster, engaged in breaking a wild mustang, has great symbolic significance. He personifies the battle of humans to tame nature in order to utilize it. Despite all resistance, professionalism and power will overcome. Soon the horse will obey human commands. This bronze statue credits man with power over nature. It also symbolizes male dominance over nature outside the home, while the woman focuses her efforts on domestic activities.

Watson, William [British, †1921]: Plowing With Oxen Teams, oil on canvas, 31.5×43.5 in., 1866, signed

Plowing with oxen is a very popular subject of 19th century paintings. This painting by Watson is a fairly typical example of this genre. Plowing with oxen was common where either the soil was too heavy to be plowed by horses, or the farmer was too poor to afford them. In this paint-ing, difficult soil conditions in a hilly countryside require six oxen. One farmhand leads the oxen while the other guides the heavy wooden plow. As in all paintings of this kind, heaven and earth are set in a romantic relationship with the cultivated and natural landscape.

Pentelei-Molnár, János [Hungarian, 1878-1924]: The Potato Harvest, oil on canvas, 31×43 in., 1901, signed

In a manner similar to the plowing theme, artists were drawn to the potato harvest. In both themes painters were fascinated with the artistic portrayal of heaven and earth. Here, too, work is the central activity. Harvesting potatoes by hand is an extraordinary physical effort, requiring all family members and temporary laborers as well. Women and children had to help with the potato harvest – not even elderly women were spared. To the left, a basket of potatoes is apparently being sold directly from the field.

Knaus, Ludwig [German, 1829-1910]: Potato Harvest, oil on panel, 33×47 in., 1879, signed

Ludwig Knaus, the famous German genre and portrait painter, depicts a family harvesting potatoes. This painting was created at a time when artists pursued themes of work in daily life. Their interest moved between romantic idealism and social realism. While the farm workers painted by Max Liebermann clearly belong to social realism, Knaus just as clearly remains in the idealistic genre manner. His *Potato Harvest* presents a good example. The colorful painting represents the man as Adam working the soil and the woman in the center responsible for the children. The little child in her arms receives the benefit of the harvest, a potato in his mouth. The other children move playfully around the field. Grandmother needs to take a rest. She has a painful hip or back. A lumber cart passes by in the background. The painting tells a story to be enjoyed by young and old alike, even though the difficult and hard side of farming life is not ignored.

**Dupré, Julien [French, 1851-1910]: Stacking Grain
Sheafs, oil on canvas, 20.5×25.2 in., signed**

The grain harvest is another example of the harvest theme, portrayed in countless paintings over the past thousand years with both men and women found in the fields. A popular representation is the combination of male cutters and female grain binders. In this picture the grain is already cut so the grain cutter returns to help with the binding. As in the famous painting *The Gleaners* by Millet, the woman wears the French national colors of blue, white and red.

Lorenz, Richard [American, 1858-1915]: Harvest Time, oil on canvas, 29×37 in., 1902, signed

Although born in Voigstädt, Weimar, Germany, Richard Lorenz arrived in Milwaukee in 1886 and spent most of his professional life in Wisconsin. He is known for his western and midwestern scenes depicting the area around his adopted city. Here he presents a Wisconsin farming scene. The man cuts the grain with a scythe while the woman binds the sheaves. This was a typical division of work between the genders at harvest time, when everyone was needed. They made maximum use of good weather to bring in the harvest. The golden color of the grain combines with the blue sky and dress of the woman to form an emotional, moving and harmonious composition.

**Seignac, Paul [French, 1826-1904]: The Cider Mill, oil
on canvas, 25×35 in., signed**

In England, France and the southwest regions of Germany, cider is a very popular beverage. The filtered sweet apple juice is fermented to produce a drink with little remaining sugar, therefore containing 4 percent alcohol. It is truly the "wine of the poor people." Seignac shows the cider pressing process, where workers extract juice from the apples. Five men turn the pushwheel to employ maximum leverage and engage the large press at right. The children are tasting the fresh apple juice, as is the woman in the center background, apparently having brought more apples in the basket on her back.

Kappis, Albert [German, 1836-1914]: **Wine Press**, oil
on paper on canvas, 11×15.5 in., 1868, signed

A press similar to that in the picture on the left is applied to the pressing of grapes for red wine. In reality, at this point in the process, the fresh juice from the red grapes does not have the full red color as indicated in this painting. The press, hewn from rough lumber, is located in a barn, and is operated by only a single worker who turns a drive screw.

Wagner-Höhenberg, Josef [German, *1870]: In the Mill, Trading Grain, oil on canvas, 28×40 in., ca. 1930

This painting represents a typical example of genre painting. One can sense the story it tells. At right, two customers very critically examine the miller's grain to determine its quality. The artist introduces a touch of ridicule by means of their body language and the inclusion of an umbrella.

He possibly expresses some disdain for the profession of the middleman or broker. The miller, however, exhibits self-confidence, and his assistant with the wooden shovel follows the scene with great interest.

Larroick, A. (?): Man With Sickle, bronze, 11 in., signed

Field workers use extreme concentration while reaping with the scythe. Handling a scythe requires a good deal of practice. Scythes have been found with fine stone edges dating back to the Stone Age. The cutting edge has to be sharpened and hardened from time to time. Whetting and hammering the scythe, similar to forging, accomplishes the hardening.

Valentin, M. [German, 19th c.]: Field Worker, Male, bronze, 11.5 in., signed

Valentin, M. [German, 19th c.]: Field Worker, Female, bronze, 11.5 in., signed

The two bronze statues by Valentin follow a typical iconographic and cultural pattern. The male figure to the left is a sower. With his right hand he evenly distributes seed, while his left hand handles the seed pouch. This activity is almost always performed by men. The female statue is a reaper, holding a sickle in her right hand and cut grain in her left hand. Wielding a sickle is historically treated as a female activity, but cutting with a larger, long-handled scythe is typically treated as male activity.

Waldmüller, Ferdinand Georg [Austrian, 1793-1865]:
Farming Girl and Hunter, bronze, 9.5 in., signed

Waldmüller portrays a young female farm laborer and young hunter as a romantic couple. The girl carries a large pitchfork on her shoulder, a symbolic reference to her standing. She is poor, a fact made clear by Waldmül-ler. She raises her dress a bit, in a provocative pose. The hunter belongs to a higher social standing as indicated by his perfect hunting outfit. Romantic liaison knows no social limits.

Chalaignon, J. [French]: Woman Carrying Sheaf of Wheat, bronze, 9.5 in., signed "J Chalaignon, France.", marked "Bronze Le Garanti al posse Titre"

This appears to be a field hand working as a sheaf binder, carrying the cut grain to the collection point. It is possible, perhaps even typical of the artists of the 19th century, that this woman is a gleaner. As a gleaner, this bronze would represent a woman of the poorest class, such as described in the Bible, permitted to collect leftover grain for her own use.

Brandt, F. [German]: Homeward Bound Field Worker, bronze, 16.5 in., 19ᵗʰ c., signed, foundrymark "Deutsche Bronze"

Cardona, José [Spanish, †1903?]: Peasant Laborer, bronze, 22 in., ca. 1903

Depicting return of workers from their daily labors is a very popular subject in art history. These two statues demonstrate the effect of heavy labor in the life of the working class. Both sculptures clearly express the exhaustion of the worker after a full day of heavy toil. The sculptors stress the generally stooped shape of body and soul as a result of the heavy, manual work performed by the seasonal farm hands and laborers.

Model of an Early Mowing Machine, brass, 10.5×15.5×9

This is a brass model of a grass mowing machine designed to be drawn by a pair of horses. The cutting blades can be folded against the carriage and are driven by gearing inside the right wheel and a transverse v-belt. Mowing machines were originally developed for cutting grain. Grass has a low cutting resistance but requires a more precise cutting mechanism. Grain mowing machines were developed around 1825. The first mowing machine for grass cutting was probably developed by Walter Abbott Wood of Hoosick Falls, New York, around 1859. An example of such a mower is pictured in the figure at right. The model in the ECKHART G. GROHMANN COLLECTION corresponds functionally to the machine Wood built.

Model of a Potato Planter, iron, 19×8.5×9 in.

The potato-planting machine is a development much later than the mowing machine. In 1913 the first prototype machines were tested with little success. Further development was added in the 1920s and particularly after World War II. The model in the ECKHART G. GROHMANN COLLECTION probably dates back to the 1920s. It is designed to be pulled by a tractor and to plant three rows of potatoes.

The seed potatoes fall through the tubes into the furrows cut by the three front blades. Four rear blades close the furrows again. Models like these two were built for patent applications, for teaching and research purposes, and for exhibitions at trade fairs. [Thanks to Dr. Hermann, *Deutsches Landwirtschaftsmuseum* (German Agricultural Museum) at Hohenheim, Germany.]

8. MISCELLANEOUS

In addition to the art in the main groupings presented thus far, the ECKHART G. GROHMANN COLLECTION contains a variety of art that will be summarized in this final chapter. Among these are outstanding paintings by such artists as Von Brueghel and Van Goyen. We also find curiosities such as Kobel's *The Unsuccessful Experiment* and rare portrayals of professions such as *The Taxidermist* by Lucas. Some other subjects are more frequently represented in the history of work related paintings. To this group belong the paintings of a dentist and all activities connected with the ocean, such as fishing, or miscellaneous harbor scenes. Although they are a relatively small portion of the collection at this point, they afford a good overview of these subjects. Among these are two famous sculptures by Constantin Meunier, whose paintings were previously described.

Even the artists themselves are represented in this chapter with four paintings portraying them as workers in their own workshops or studios. After all, the painter's profession is to a large extent a trade, and numerous painters' studios in the past were workshops with many employees to produce pictures for the market. One needs only to think of Rembrandt or the Brueghel family.

School of Rembrandt [Dutch, second quarter 17th c.]:
The Rat Catcher, oil on panel, 15.5×10 in.

Not only in the style and colors, but also in its view of the subject matter, this painting *The Rat Catcher* represents a typical Dutch painting of the 17th century. Rembrandt himself composed a drawing and an etching of this subject. A student in his workshop executed this painting in oil on oak panel using the available wood panels, paints and brushes of the Rembrandt workshop. Many artists were held in poor social esteem and barely made a modest living. Thus, driven by artists' needs, barbers, country village teachers, farmers, bakers, etc., were now respectable enough to be portrayed in oil paintings, if they could pay. Here a rat catcher offers his services – a very useful service with the looming threat of black plague. Hanging from his trap are skins of rats for sale. On his shoulder sits a ferret he uses to stir up rats. The man at the door is probably poor and may even be blind. He carries his right arm in a sling and doesn't seem to have the money needed to hire the rat catcher.

Vibert, Jehan Georges [French, 1840-1902]: Polishing Day, oil on panel, 18.5×15.25 in., signed

Today is cleaning day in the monastery. A devoted monk is committed to perfection as he polishes all of the monastery's precious metal objects to their highest luster. The monk takes the opportunity of useful work and combines it with the enjoyment of a sunbath. This is a typical genre painting, communicating a story to the observer that brings a smile to his face.

Van Goyen, Jan Josefsz [Dutch, 1596-1656]: A River Landscape with Lime-Kilns, oil on panel, 14.8×20 in., monogrammed "vg"

Nature commonly provides limestone (calcium carbonate) in large quantities for use as a raw material, especially for cement, coloring and fertilizer, as well as a blast furnace ingredient to produce pig iron. By heating the limestone to about 1000 °C, the carbon escapes as carbon dioxide leaving lime for further processing. With the addition of water, the lime becomes the raw material base for mortar. In the kiln the limestone is heated to a thoroughly red glow. This is best accomplished by crushing the limestone into small pieces and placing them onto iron grating exposed to a fire below. The fire is fed by wood, charcoal or hard coal. This burning process takes several days. After it is cooled, the lime is removed from the bottom of the kiln.

Van Goyen, Jan Josefsz.: Landscape with Lime-Kilns, sketch, 1627; Staatliches Museum Schwerin, Inv.No. 1254

Lime kilns have existed for a long time. Yet today ancient lime kiln ruins are found only in Europe. This painting by Van Goyen and that following by Kratzer are two exceptional examples of a multitude of pictures with the lime kiln theme. While Kratzer portrays a plain, but very impressive kiln in operation, the Van Goyen painting is much more detailed. In a typical Dutch landscape that he painted so many times, Van Goyen shows two kilns and their supporting structures located next to a river. A worker carries a bag of limestones up to the charging area. Tools needed for the removal of the finished lime are seen leaning against the kiln wall. Two of these tools also can be recognized in the painting by Kratzer. The physical labor to charge the kiln is clearly portrayed in the Van Goyen painting.

Kratzer, Karl [German, 1827-1903]: Lime Kiln, oil on canvas, 10.5×14 in., 1847, signed

Karl Kratzer painted a lime kiln operating as they have since the dark ages. The fire shines through the door of the brick kiln, and smoke escapes to the sky. Two long-handled tools to the right of the door are used to scrape the lime out of the kiln after firing. No workers are visible, since there is little to do during the firing process, which lasts for several days. Kratzer, along with many other artists, was probably intrigued by the ancient appearance of this technology. Another attribute is the combination of the colors white, blue and red, as relating to the tricolor French and United States flags.

Pratt, Jonathan [British, 1835-1911]: James Watt's Workshop, oil on canvas, 16.5×20 in., 1889, signed

Scottish engineer James Watt (1736-1819) substantially improved the steam engine designed by Newcomen in 1711. Newcomen's engine introduced a jet of cold water into the engine to condense the steam. Unfortunately, the water also cooled the piston and other metal parts, making it necessary to reheat them during the next cycle. By moving the condenser away from the piston, Watt increased the engine's efficiency by almost 75 percent.

He patented his invention in 1769 and installed the first operating engine in a coal mine. Over the next few years Watt's engines entirely replaced Newcomen's engines. While not the inventor of steam engines, Watt's contributions led to its common use. Following Watt's death, his private workshop was preserved just as he had left it in Heathfield, England. The workshop is painted here by Jonathan Pratt, some 70 years after Watt's death.

Brueghel, Pieter, the Younger [Dutch, 1564-1638]: The Peasant Lawyer, oil on panel, 28×41 in.

This painting by Pieter Brueghel the Younger was so popular that a hundred or more versions may have been produced, although certainly not by Brueghel himself. The painting appears under different titles, such as *The Tax Collector* and *Payment of the Tithes*. However, experts agree that this portrayal is of a village attorney, composed with satirical intent.

When this painting was created in the 17th century, attorneys did not enjoy a good reputation. They were considered to be corrupt "twisters of the law," but because they were needed, they wielded tremendous power. The painter attempts to ridicule the lawyers by employing caricature to gain a small measure of satisfaction.

A number of village people come before the village attorney to get advice and representation in various legal matters. Humbly they approach his desk. They are fearfully crowded together. The poor villagers cannot pay the demanded fee in cash and offer instead their own products: grapes, eggs and a slaughtered chicken. The lawyer endlessly studies a document that apparently involves a legal matter of a client to the far right. It seems clear that the matter will not be settled in favor of the client. Untouched by their plight, he lets the group of farmers wait. Papers are spread throughout the office. At first glance they seem to be pending cases.

The office scribe in the left background seems to be totally overwhelmed, which is no wonder considering his apparently modest preparation. Far to the left of the picture stands an isolated and frightened man. He seems to have great apprehension for the lawyer's authority. This world of written paperwork and legal files is totally alien to him. Another man to the left of the lawyer studies a wall calendar in great amazement. The red sand hourglass on the lawyer's table can be seen as a common baroque symbol of fleeting time, perhaps an early reference to charging by the hour.

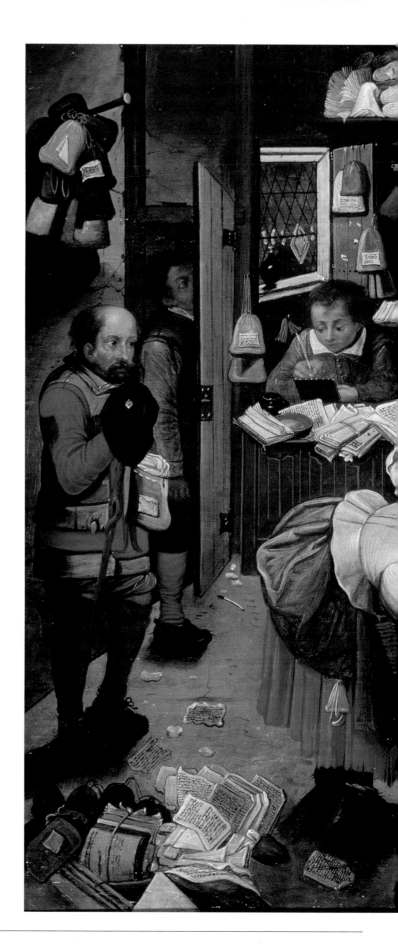

**Helmont, Mattheus von [Dutch, 1623-after 1674]:
An Alchemist With Assistants in a Laboratory, oil on
canvas, 23×33 in., signed**

The painter provides a view into an alchemist's laboratory, normally closed to outsiders. He employs no fewer than 10 assistants. Large laboratories were not a rare subject and nearly a hundred years earlier Strandanus had painted such a laboratory. In the center sits the alchemist. He is in the midst of examining a recently prepared chemical mixture. On his lap is a reference book with the typical symbols of an alchemist's secret knowledge. On the left page, for example, a circle with a dot serves as symbol for the sun and for gold, while a growing quarter moon is the symbol for the moon and for silver. On the right page of his book are the symbols for copper and lead, among others. Perhaps this alchemist is trying to synthesize gold, as were so many alchemists at that time. His well-equipped laboratory depicts him as a very busy man. While most of the assistants are busy executing various assignments, the one in front of his chair unwraps additional reference books. This painting does not imply a satirical character, as did many others of the day. Rather, it expresses the high regard for science that prevailed during the baroque age.

Kobell, Ferdinand [German, 1740-1799]: Unsuccessful Experiment, oil on canvas, 15×18 in., 1775, monogrammed

Since the 16th century there have been many caricatures of alchemists. Kobell, otherwise known as a landscape artist, paints an unsuccessful experiment in the style of older Dutch paintings. A vessel with diverse ingredients explodes just after heating on the oven. This picture can be seen as homage to the art of the 16th century, as well as a criticism of the credence given to the science of this time. While the scientist is terribly frightened, another person looks on from the doorway appearing merely annoyed.

**Follower of Wijck, Thomas [Dutch]: An Astronomer,
oil on panel, 19×15.5 in., 17th c.**

The 16th and 17th centuries were important periods in European astronomy. Copernicus, Kepler and Galileo revolutionized the concept of the world and its place in the universe. Astronomy was not a science purely for knowledge. Rather, it had immediate practical value, especially related to the navigation of ships. This painting shows a lovable portrait of a lonely scientist taking measurements with his dividers. On the floor is a model of the planet's paths, and behind the globe is a map indicating a connection between astronomy and geography.

Drost, Willem [Dutch, ca. 1625-ca. 1660]: Geographer, oil on panel, 29×23 in., signed as "Rembrandt van Rijn"

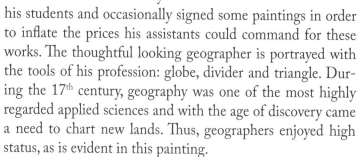

This painting carries a Rembrandt van Rijn signature, which was probably done by Drost himself. The contemporary nature of the signature has been confirmed by the painting's restorer. Drost is known to have inscribed the Rembrandt signature on other paintings, for example, *Portrait of a Young Man* in the *Wallace Collection*, London. He has employed the typical light-dark painting techniques of the master. Students in the Rembrandt workshop used the same paint mixes and other supplies as the master. Legend has it that Rembrandt put final touches on works by his students and occasionally signed some paintings in order to inflate the prices his assistants could command for these works. The thoughtful looking geographer is portrayed with the tools of his profession: globe, divider and triangle. During the 17th century, geography was one of the most highly regarded applied sciences and with the age of discovery came a need to chart new lands. Thus, geographers enjoyed high status, as is evident in this painting.

**Gerard, Thomas [Belgian, 1663-1720]: Studio of a
Painter and Sculptor, oil on canvas, 33×46.5 in.**

The view of the observer is directed toward the master
artist at his stand-up desk by the window, affording him
the best daylight conditions. The center portrays the well-
proportioned arrangement of his various works of art. The
depth of the room is emphasized by a bombastically folded
curtain. In the center of the painting is an oil lamp stand,
indicating the master sometimes works at night. At the
lower right corner is an array of broken pieces, probably an
unsuccessful workpiece. Behind that are a hollowed stone
with an oil carafe, and tools to grind and prepare color
paints. Two groups of students are in deep discussions.
The youngest student seems to be lacking the necessary
commitment; he escaped from the workshop and tries to
reconnect with the group through the little window at the
upper right. The globe in the center is intended to depict
the universal talent of the master. The sculpture pointing
out of the window symbolizes the faraway dreams of the
master.

Pepino, Anton Josef [Austrian, 1863-1921]: Sculptor
Viktor Tilgner in His Studio, oil on panel, 19×27.5 in.,
1889, signed

The well-known Austrian sculptor Viktor Tilgner is portrayed working in his studio along with two of his assistants. Tilgner produced a multitude of busts. Among them were two monumental busts, one of Mozart and another of the industrialist Josef Werndl in Steyr. This painting honors his work three years after his death.

Seitz, Anton [German, 1829-1900]: The Portrait Painter, oil on panel, 12.5×17.5 in., signed

The landlord is having his portrait painted. The bridle hanging down from the left of the wall suggests a function of a mail-coach driver. Some bread and new wine upon the cask to his left elbow help him recover from the strain of the recent journey. The artist is holding a palette with the required paints in his left hand. His progress is being followed by all family members with rapt attention. The bundle containing old documents is meant to underscore the significance of the landlord's position. The great-grandmother seems to be quite content with the progress of the painting, while her great-grandchild is displaying a somewhat sceptical expression. On the top of the table to the right is a steaming dish containing a warm meal, as well as a jar and a glass of new wine. The artist's paintbox has been thoroughly inspected by the youngest grandchild, who has just made a find with a tube of paint, which she is trying to squeeze out at the moment. Her elder brother is expectantly watching the outcome of her efforts.

Kinzel, Joseph [Austrian, 1852-1925]: Returning to the Studio, oil on canvas, 21×18 in., signed

An artist's studio is shown in an attic. The painter has just returned home with his dachshund. Could this be a self-portrait? An iron oven is the only means of supplying a little heat to the room. Several watercolor paintings hang about the area. The oven seems capable of roasting so a wider range of meals can be prepared. No exhaust hood is evident, but there is plenty of ventilation. The roof itself does not inspire a great deal of confidence. A few earthen pottery items and some paintings are depicted at the right. The artist holds a framed canvas in his right hand and carries his easel in his left hand.

Betz, Ernst [German, 1898-1989]: The Only Gem Polisher of Munich, oil on canvas, 17.5×23.5 in., 1950, signed

Precious and semiprecious stones receive their decorative appearance with cutting and grinding. For thousands of years people have adorned themselves with colored stones. The polisher of precious stones shown in this painting works with great concentration to give a ruby a final polishing. His electrically-driven polishing wheel turns in a water bath. With his right hand he regulates the speed of the rotating disc. The magnifying glass in the foreground allows him to monitor the quality of his work as he progresses.

Beckert, Oskar [German, *1878]: The Piano Maker at the Piano Key Manufacturing, oil on panel, 23.5×19.5

Keyed musical instruments have been used since the 16th century. However, the piano mechanism of activating the hammer with only a key was developed in just the 18th century. The piano builder in this painting divides selected wood pieces with a large cutting knife to produce the rough blanks for piano keys. He appears relaxed, smoking his pipe and concentrating on his work.

Mart, Alfons: Splendid Goldsmith's Workshop, oil on canvas, 35.5×28 in., signed

This storytelling painting brings us into the goldsmith's workshop that is fully equipped. A great variety of tools, anvils, vices, tongs, pliers, files and forging hammers in various sizes are displayed. A cloth is suspended underneath the workbench to catch any chips or minute pieces of precious metals. One goldsmith critically examines a workpiece while the other reaches for a tool and casts an admiring glance at his colleague's work.

Krug, Andreas: The Old Violin-Maker in His Workshop, oil on canvas, 27.5×23.5 in., signed

The first musical instruments based on a bow and string were probably used in India. Arab traders brought them to Europe in the Middle Ages. Violins have been built in Italy since the 16th century. This instrument builder seems to specialize in violas, but violins and a lute are also evident in his shop. Building these instruments is a highly skilled art.

**Welke, Ralf [German, *1962]: Basketmaker, oil on
canvas, 20×23.5 in., signed**

Basket weaving is an ancient trade still in existence. Pliable willow tree branches are used. The rods are cut in spring and soaked in water to make them more pliable, as seen in the painting above. The bark is peeled off with special tongs. Weaving begins at the bottom with a so-called rod cross base. Vertical rods are fastened to that base and the side wall is built on them.

Heim, D.: Print Shop, oil on canvas, 22×27.5 in.

Heim paints a printer's workshop in the middle of the 19th century. At the left, the typesetter sits next to his letter type box containing the lead letters. The printing machine is a steam-driven mechanical printing press for duplex print, equipped with a pressure cylinder. It is capable of printing 800-1000 sheets per hour. These presses have been available since about 1810, first driven by water or steam power and later by electricity. An operator must feed each sheet of paper manually into the press. The master printer stands on a platform and critically inspects a finished sheet. [Thanks to the *Landesmuseum für Technik und Arbeit in Mannheim.*]

Lucas, John Templeton [British, 1836-1860]: The
Taxidermist, oil on canvas, 19×15.5 in., 1874

A taxidermist carefully inspects his newest creation. He has mounted a small green parakeet on its perch. He still holds the paintbrush with which he painted the base. To the left are several dead birds, apparently waiting to be prepared and mounted. The professional mounting of animals by taxidermists serves the sciences and teaching professions even to this day. It also finds application in the home as, for example, hunting and fishing trophies.

**Horemans, Jan Josef [Dutch, 1682-1759]: A Dentist's
Surgery, oil on canvas, 15.5×12.5 in.**

Two hundred years ago, the local barber also served as the dentist. In this scene the barber removes a problem tooth from the patient's gums by means of a pair of tongs. A woman, apparently a member of the patient's family, says a prayer in an attempt to alleviate his suffering. A boy in the foreground is seeking solace on a woman's lap. An elderly neighbor walking by the hairdresser's shop appears to be getting a great deal of pleasure out of this event, which he also must have experienced. A collection of ointment pots and flasks containing various tinctures can be seen on the table.

**Piltz, Otto [German, 1846-1910]: Women Splicing
Feathers, oil on canvas, 25×36 in., 1877, signed on the
right bag "Theresienstift Weimar"**

Stripping feathers is not physically strenuous, but it is quite a dusty occupation. In this scene feathers lie in abundance on the floor, benches and tables. The woman in the foreground is pushing feathers down tightly into a pot. Other vessels contain stripped feather quills, many of which cover the floor.

Anonymous: Women Making Corks for Wine Bottles,
oil on canvas, 23×29 in., 19th **c.**

Bottle corks are made from the inner bark of the cork tree. The cork is especially suitable for sealing wine bottles because it can breathe and permits a minute exchange of gas with the outer air. This painting shows a cork manufacturing shop with an all-female staff performing the manual labor. The apparently strict supervisor is the only male. The women sit on workbenches and finish the rough-cut cork pieces. The painter is less interested in the details of their work, which he does not depict, than in the layout, structure and atmosphere of the workshop.

Stoll, J. [Austrian]: Vegetable Trader, oil on canvas, 16×20 in., signed

In addition to fresh fruits and vegetables, this trader apparently offers pickled fruits and vegetables out of his numerous glazed earthen pots and carafes. His red nose provides ample evidence of the alcohol content in his products, which are all preserved in alcohol. A cask, a pail and several other vessels containing preserved vegetables are at the left of the picture. A couple of covered bottles across the room suggest some interesting contents.

Nikutowski, Arthur Johann Severin [German, 1830-1888]: **At the Fair**, oil on canvas on plywood, 25×40 in., 1882, signed

A small German town about 200 years ago celebrates a fair. Many different showmen have gathered to produce this event. A show trailer occupies the foreground of the painting. Such a trailer is equipped with a heating system and provides a cosy home for the entertainers. A fair of this type with its particular merchandise could last for several days, so the migrant fair workers need to do their wash. A local policeman wearing a spiked helmet and a white leather belt is berating a couple of romping children. The showman has retired to his trailer and is warming up with a hot beverage while his wife and their children are busy dealing with their laundry. A temporary shelter has been set up at the inn next door to accommodate the guests' animals. In the courtyard, a great deal of commotion is caused by the simultaneous feeding of the horses, the parking of the carriages, and the arrival of new riders. The riders tapping against the window of the guesthouse are rewarded with a snifter of schnapps. On the inn's porch, several guests have assembled to enjoy the hustle and bustle of the crowd in the market square.

Pfeiffer, Otto [German, 1882-1955]: Ice Block Transport, oil on canvas, 22.5×29 in., signed

The picturesque scenery includes a frozen lake in a kettle moraine providing ice for cooling purposes during the next summer. The blocks are loaded onto a transport sled drawn by a team of horses. The ice blocks will be stored in large barns, and covered with sawdust and straw to insulate them against the warmth of the approaching summer. The ice blocks are sold to households and the food industry to refrigerate food and raw materials. During the second half of the 20th century, electric refrigeration equipment replaced this basic industry. The old descriptive word "ice-box" still survives, now referring to a refrigerator.

**Müller, Fritz [German, 1907-1999]: Geologic Drilling
Station, oil on cardboard, 31.5×28.0 in., 1957, signed**

This picture illustrates a drilling operation, apparently to determine the geological structure of the underlying layers. The objective may be oil, groundwater or minerals. Several pieces of pipe are available to produce a pipeline. To the right, a worker forges a part for the piping connection. Behind him is a small fire.

Storck, Abraham [Dutch, ca. 1635-1710?]: Negotiating Merchants at Gibraltar, oil on panel, 23×32.5 in.

The artist Abraham Storck is a very famous marine painter. He painted ships, harbors and sea battles in a variety of ways. When he painted scenes around the Mediterranean Sea, he often creatively assembled Mediterranean landscapes and architecture together into interesting pictures. The Strait of Gibraltar connects the Mediterranean Sea to the Atlantic Ocean and separates Europe from the African continent. This was one of the land routes to Asia that produced meetings of diverse cultures in the 17th century. This painting depicts active trading underway at the foot of a Moorish castle from the Middle Ages. The traders are probably Portuguese and Turkish merchants accompanied by their servants. The servants are pictured as smaller in stature to symbolize their lower rank. Several packages are transferred. The merchants' vessels carry cannons, primarily for protection against pirates. Judging from the flags, the first ship is Turkish and the second, in the rear, is a Portuguese ship. [Thanks to Ralf Stelter, Hattingen.]

Anonymous [Dutch]: Stevedores Loading Sail Ships, oil on canvas, 29×39 in., 18th c.

Due to their displacement and depth of keel, sailing ships could not get close to shore. Thus, their cargo needed to be transferred to smaller boats and taken to and from shore. The vessel at the center is under sail and leaving its mooring. In the foreground, several stevedores are unloading barrels from the small boats and reloading those boats with new transfer cargo.

Wagner, Cornelius [German, 1870-1956]: Unloading of SS King Edward on the Tyne, oil on canvas, 38.5×59 in., signed

A steam ship named King Edward is unloading a shipment of lumber. No ship of that name has yet been found, so the name may be a case of artistic license. The two lifeboats indicate this ship would have a cargo capacity of at least 1000 tons. The steamship is grounded at low tide in an eastern, or perhaps a southern, English harbor. Logs, probably imported from Finland, are unloaded with the help of boom and tackle. The logs are either tied together to form rafts and pulled by tugboats into the interior of the country, or they are loaded onto the red-sailed barges indigenous to Thames, Medway, or other harbors in eastern England. [Thanks to Dr. Scholl, *Deutsches Schiffahrtsmuseum Bremerhaven.*]

Poetzsch, Paul [German, 1858-1936]: The Net Patchers, oil on canvas, 28×39 in., 1906, signed

Two fishermen, perhaps a grandfather and grandson, sit in the sunlight mending their nets in front of a hut with a variety of fishing equipment. They employ a type of knitting needle to accomplish their task. These fishing nets must be repaired frequently since they get torn on plants and other objects when retrieved. Many artists frequently painted this quiet and relaxing activity. Max Liebermann created a large painting of this type titled *The Netmenders*.

Feyen-Perrin, François Nicolas Augustin [French, 1826-1888]: Returning Mussel Maids, oil on canvas, 16×20 in., signed

A large number of mussel gatherers return from the sandy, shallow flats now covered by the rising tide of the sea. The edible mussels are an especially popular food on the European Atlantic coast. Three attractive young ladies, well aware of the attention they receive, lead the returning crowd of mussel maids and their followers. The mild sunlight immerses the scene in many colors. Such scenes of work at the coast were very popular in the 19th century, especially in France and Holland.

Meunier, Constantin-Emile [Belgian, 1831-1905]: Bust of a Longshoreman, bronze, 22.5 in., inscribed "Anvers"

This double page features a return once again to Constantin Meunier. Although his primary interest was mining, many other trades and occupations were not overlooked in his work. As important as the iron and steel industry was for Belgium, activities connected to the sea played an important role as well. Stevedores and fishermen were of utmost importance to the Belgian economy, and therefore also to Meunier. He found in them exponents of the modern industrial workers of his time. In his characteristic manner, he combined simplicity with pride in his sculptures of stevedores and fishermen. All three works in the ECKHART G. GROHMANN COLLECTION have the stylistic

Meunier, Constantin-Emile [Belgian, 1831-1905]: Oostende Fisherman, bronze, 32.5 in., signed

form of monuments. This is especially true for the most famous bust of the stevedore from Antwerp, inscribed "Anvers." With a challenging expression on his face, this figure commands respect and honor.

Meunier, Constantin-Emile [Belgian, 1831-1905]: Longshoreman, bronze, 15 in., signed

Kalish, Max [American, 1891-1945]: Carrier, bronze, 19 in., signed, foundrymark "Meroni-Radice cire perdue Paris"

A generation later, American Max Kalish also created a series of worker sculptures, among them another stevedore type. In this piece Kalish demonstrated the movement of the body carrying an object, maybe a glass pane. In contrast to Meunier, Kalish placed increased emphasis on the male anatomy.

**Mercker, Erich [German, 1891-1973]: Rubber Rolling
Mill, Nuremberg, Germany, oil on cardboard, 15×19 in.,
signed**

In the middle of the manufacturing bay is a rubber cylinder driven by huge geared wheels. The exhaust duct at the center of the hall provides the required fresh air. In the foreground stands a motor with a cage armature. A rubber cylinder is a rolling mill where rubber is rolled to the size of sheets.

Tylle, Hans Dieter [German, *1954]: Anchor Drill Rig in the Salt-Mine, Hering, oil on canvas, 27.5×47 in., signed

This scene depicts the underground mining of salt using an anchor boring machine. Timber is not used for the support of underground salt mine shafts. The anchor installed by the drilling supports the ceiling during the daily operations, resisting any collapse. This is a very efficient operation requiring only one worker to operate the machine.

Pollak, Zsigmond [Hungarian, 1837-1912]: Workers Negotiating With Boss, oil on canvas, 32.5×48 in., 1872, signed

In this painting wage negotiations are taking place in an almost familylike environment. The side of the owner is located to the left of the table, represented by two elderly gentlemen. Behind them is a younger person, obviously a member of the family of the company owner or perhaps an engineer. The workers are depicted on the right side of the painting. To the right foreground, tools and casks can be seen that refer to the working environment of the people concerned. The high number of hammers deliberately placed in the foreground clearly indicates this is a forge.

The tongs on the wall are hollow round tools used for the processing of mostly round bars. The blacksmith standing to the right in the background is trying to expound his interests by displaying dramatic motions in a fighting spirit, while his workmates in front of him appear to be feeling bored to tears. The elderly blacksmith foreman dominating the foreground of the painting seems to know exactly what he wants, and also how to best represent the interests of both parties to try and negotiate a fair agreement.

**Ten Kate, Herman Frederik Carel [Dutch, 1822-1891]:
The Treasure Chest, oil on panel, 23.5×36.5 in., signed**

A host of armed people has taken possession of the lobby of a palatial mansion. The scene depicts the pursuit of a contribution. In the middle, two men dragging a heavy treasure chest are being instructed with a peremptory gesture by a field captain as to where they are meant to deposit the chest. The elegantly dressed mayor is about to surrender the key to the town, in a humble manner. Behind him is the town elder councilman who has also adopted a humble attitude. The scene is dominated by the armed men. To the left in the foreground is a soldier bearing a musket. The flag of the occupying forces is resting in the corner to the left. Just in front at the top of a shelf, a helmet can be seen. Two intimidated citizens are in front of the flag. The musketeer has fastened several charges for his musket to his back strap.

INDEX OF ARTISTS

German-English Academy Building, 1020 N. Broadway, Milwaukee
Future Home of the ECKHART G. GROHMANN COLLECTION
A Short History

The *German-English Academy* building has served as the home of two major educational institutions – the *German-English Academy* and *Milwaukee School of Engineering* – both major forces in the educational landscape of the city of Milwaukee and beyond.

Mid-19th century Milwaukee was one of the most German-populated cities in America, with at least a third of its population comprised of German immigrants or their children. German businessmen headed major beer brewing, tanning and manufacturing operations.

Dissatisfied with the state of the school system and teacher training available in the United States, Milwaukee's German settlers decided to take action to provide quality education for children that equaled or exceeded that in Europe.

In May 1851, they began a Milwaukee Schulverein (*Milwaukee Educational Association*) and soon after formally established the *German-English Academy*, with Peter Engelman as director. A formalized, teacher-training institution came to fruition, but Engelman died in 1874 before seeing his dream of a national teachers seminary in Milwaukee come true. In 1878, the newly formed *National German-American Teachers Seminary* made the *German-English Academy* its home, drawing prospective teachers from around the country and, in turn, providing the school with excellent teachers. The teachers who were educated there became the backbone of the *Milwaukee Public School System,* as well as schools throughout the country. Another group, the Normal School of Gymnastics of the *North American Gymnastics Union* also called the academy home.

With the growth of the academy, seminary and gymnastics training enterprises, a new facility was needed. Elizabeth Pfister, widow of tanning magnate and hotelier Guido Pfister, and their daughter, Mrs. Louise Vogel, gave money and land for a new facility to the academy. A five-story cream city brick, stone and terra-cotta building was constructed on Broadway and dedicated on April 30, 1891. The building is of late Gothic Revival and Renaissance style featuring stone and terra-cotta ornaments and arcades of two-story arched windows. The following year a nearly identical building for the gymnastics union was built adjacent to the first, and the two were connected. This second building had the words

"Turnlehrer" (gymnastics teacher) Seminar N.A.T.B. (*North American Turners Building*) on it, and it contained a state-of-the art gymnasium on the first floor with a 27-foot ceiling height that could accommodate gymnastics.

The building even has ties to the renowned *Milwaukee Public Museum*, as it served as a museum for the collection of the *Natural History Society of Wisconsin*, founded in 1852 by Peter Engelman. The society donated its substantial collection of specimens of flora and fauna of Wisconsin to the city in 1882 as the nucleus for a public museum, hence establishing the *Milwaukee Public Museum.*

In 1932, *Milwaukee School of Engineering* (MSOE) bought the building, forming the foundation for the permanent campus of the ever-growing university. The *German-English Academy* was designated a city landmark in 1973 because of its significant role in education in Milwaukee. In 1977 it was added to the *National Register of Historic Places.* In 1980, the cost of needed repairs to the building became prohibitive, and MSOE sold the building to a development group that refurbished it and made it into rental offices.

Mr. Grohmann recently acquired the building with the intent of providing a suitable home for his extensive "Man at Work" collection on the campus of MSOE.